PLANNING AND CITIES

General Editor

GEORGE R. COLLINS, Columbia University

P9-BJL-186

1. Frederick Law Olmsted (1822–1903); woodcut portrait ca. 1893.

Frederick Law Olmsted and the American Environmental Tradition

ALBERT FEIN

George Braziller   New York

To the Memory of My Father
Samuel William Fein
(1902–1959)

Frederick Law Olmsted ". . . belongs before all else to the generation in which he is born. We want men of height and breadth and purity, and a Nation's wants produce their own fulfillment." (Katherine P. Wormeley, *The United States Sanitary Commission*)

CONTENTS

GENERAL EDITOR'S PREFACE

The name of Frederick Law Olmsted, Sr. has begun to receive once more the attention it has long deserved.

At the time Olmsted was involved in the design of environments and urban amenities in the late nineteenth century, his contemporaries—professional and public alike—seem to have been well aware of his pivotal role in the shaping and preserving of our American heritage. But his work merged so imperceptibly into the fabric of our towns, cities, suburbs, and countryside that later generations assumed that their surroundings had been endowed by nature itself, and Olmsted's accomplishments were overlooked if not forgotten. Today a group of scholars, with our author in foremost rank, has rediscovered what Olmsted did for us; they are chronicling and illustrating his accomplishments for the benefit of the new environmentalists—for many of whose ideals Olmsted is the prototype.

The intention of the series of books with which this volume is associated is to provide pictorial and historical data on aspects of cities and planning for the edification of both students and laymen. With this in mind, Dr. Fein has included here generous bibliographies, source lists, and chronological inventories for those interested in pursuing the problems that concerned Olmsted. The illustrations make up what is probably the most complete representation to date of Olmsted's projects; they have been arranged in a thematic fashion, so as to acquaint the reader with the various categories of Olmsted's design activity.

Happily this book, planned several years ago, emerges in the sesquicentennial year of Olmsted's birth and thus can do homage to one of the great figures of frontier and city during America's nineteenth century. One of the strengths of Albert Fein's text is that it articulates the function Olmsted assumed as an effective reformist, from his early analysis of the circumstances that produced the lot of the nation's black people, to his later tussles in the rough-and-tumble of New York City politics. It makes clear his lifelong goal of improving the immediate environment of those who, through choice or necessity, live in the American city.

G. R. C.

PREFACE

Since our interpretation of the past is always influenced by the times in which we live, it is not surprising that an increased interest in the life and work of Frederick Law Olmsted is now taking place. In less than a decade, many of his more important publications have been reissued; several doctoral dissertations about him have been completed; additional graduate research on specialized aspects of his career is being carried on; a number of full-length biographies are in progress; and, most significantly, his varied contributions to American civilization are being incorporated in a more familiar way into general historical literature and his name more popularly identified with the many projects he planned and designed. In sum, Olmsted is gradually being rediscovered and reinterpreted as a major figure in the American experience—comparable, on numerous levels, to such persons as William Penn, Thomas Jefferson, and Benjamin Franklin.

There are many reasons for this renaissance, but central to it, certainly, is the relevance of his life experiences and planning contributions to the three major crises undergone by this nation during the last decade—racial, urban, and ecological. Olmsted developed theories and proposed projects which remain as viable physical and visual elements—integral parts of the social fabric, affecting the lives of millions of citizens. In this book, which is an effort to define, explain, and illustrate the meaning of some of his contributions, the social and physical aspects of his work are considered as one—as, in fact, he approached the environment.

If this book helps to clarify the total meaning of Olmsted's work —not only with respect to parks, but in terms of the total national experience—it will have more than served its purpose. If it strengthens our perception that America has a tradition of environmental planning and design that perhaps has not been sufficiently appreciated and understood before, it will have gone beyond what any scholar reasonably has a right to expect.

No written appreciation can ever adequately express my debt to the following institutions and to the dedicated professionals who make scholarly work possible. In the Manuscript Division of the Library of Congress I was aided by Carolyn H. Sung, Charles Cooney, and John Valley. I am grateful, as well, to William H. Bond, Librarian, and Carolyn E. Jakeman, Assistant Librarian for Reference, of the Houghton Library, Harvard University; to Paul R. Rugan, Keeper of the Manuscripts, and Jean McNeice, of the Manuscript Division of the New York Public Library; to James J. Heslin, Director; James Gregory, Librarian; and Thomas J. Dunnings, Jr., of the Manuscript Division of The New-York Historical Society; and to Thelma Mielke, Reference Librarian, the Brooklyn Center, Long Island University.

For illustrations, I am indebted to Caroline Shillaber, Librarian of the Graduate School of Design, Harvard University, and to her staff: Patricia Obst and Bronwyn Hurd; to Wilson Duprey of The New-York Historical Society; to the staff of the Garden Library, The Dumbarton Oaks Library, Washington, D.C.; to Albert K. Baragwanath, Curator of Portraits and Prints of The Museum of the City of New York; to Elizabeth Roth, Keeper of Prints, The Prints Division of the New York Public Library; to the staff of the Photo Service Division of that institution; and to the staff of the Chicago Historical Society. I deeply appreciate the assistance of the public libraries of Detroit, Louisville, Lynn (Massachusetts), and Boston. In addition, I am grateful to Thomas M. Paine, who photographed the plan of the Robert Treat Paine home.

Throughout my work I have been fortunate to have had the understanding and assistance of friends and colleagues. Among those who have read and offered criticism of the manuscript are Milton W. Brown, Chairman, Department of Art, the Graduate

Center, the City University of New York; George R. Collins, Department of Art History and Archaeology, Columbia University, who commissioned this work as General Editor of the series; James M. Fitch, School of Architecture, Columbia University; Elliott Gatner, Department of History, Long Island University; Milton M. Klein, Department of History, University of Tennessee; and Laura W. Roper, the principal Olmsted scholar, through whose work and generosity many have gained knowledge, insight, and—not less than these—friendship. I have been fortunate in having had the opportunity to explore some of the ideas developed in this book with students of the Department of Landscape Architecture, Harvard University.

In addition, I deeply appreciate the contributions of three people, two of whom, while not having read this manuscript, have had a particular role in its evolution: first, the late Richard Hofstadter, my doctoral adviser, who always encouraged me in the direction of my work; second, Lewis Mumford, whose writings first heightened my interest in the subject and with whom I am fortunate to have been able to discuss my work; and, finally, my wife, who has not only read and reviewed every single word of this manuscript, but who has had to carry much of the burden of managing a home and caring for two children, to whom no expression of thanks is adequate. For any misinterpretations or errors of fact, I alone, of course, am responsible.

ALBERT FEIN

Long Island University
November, 1971

Frederick Law Olmsted and the American Environmental Tradition

I

THE HISTORIC CONTEXT OF ENVIRONMENT

Frederick Law Olmsted (1822–1903), this nation's most comprehensive environmental planner and designer, contributed to the development of cities and regions, of a national park system, and of the United States Forest Service. It was always with a commitment to social democracy that he completed his prototypical designs for such planned environments as urban parks, parkways, suburban communities, and campuses. His work, or examples of his influence, are still evident in every region of this country and in Canada.

Born in the rural environs of Hartford, Connecticut, on April 26, 1822, Olmsted was a member of an old New England family that had ties to the land and the sea. The village provided a communal basis of life, but the age was one of constant change. The certainty of the past with its traditions was being shattered. Protestant fundamentalism was under assault by science; the Anglo-Saxon homogeneity of the nation was disappearing; an agrarian-commercial economic base was giving way to one founded on

3

industrialization; and the institution of slavery was increasingly found to be in violation of all that a democratic nation was or wished to be.

These social and economic changes created the setting for the emergence of heroic-tragic personalities. Indeed, heroism was a widely respected nineteenth-century ideal with which Olmsted identified through his readings in the works of the English historian Thomas Carlyle and the American philosopher Ralph Waldo Emerson.[1] The heroic quality of Olmsted's own life is manifested in his many large-scale and varied attempts to meet the fundamental challenges to the nation's future posed by rapid urbanization and related social problems.

The tragic element in his life was the suffering he experienced in pursuit of his aims and the degree to which his theories and solutions failed to be accepted. As the privileged eldest son of a wealthy merchant and the product of an incomplete home life, Olmsted seemed to need personal success very badly. Frustration with the making of public policy brought him great anguish. During his lifetime he was to suffer at least two breakdowns brought on by physical exhaustion and mental stress, and his last five years were spent in a mental hospital. However, his anguish, although heightened by the deaths of a brother and son whom he loved dearly, never—until the last illness—diminished his commitments, efforts, or imaginative qualities as environmental planner and designer. Indeed, personal trauma seemed, somehow, to enhance them.[2]

Olmsted's varied contributions are best understood as the product of a completely engaged personality whose life experiences spanned the greater part of the nineteenth century. His professional career as an environmental planner was shaped by a principal concern of nineteenth-century intellectuals: the creation of a unifying national culture.[3] Olmsted's response to the main question of how to plan an American environment shifted during and after the Civil War from local and decentralized to regional and centralized institutions and forms. However, the humane and scientific purposes of his planning remained constant; only the scale and aesthetic expression of some of his designs altered dramatically.

4

Two factors exacerbated this tension between goals and forms. The first was the subordination of the humanitarian and scientific aspirations of Olmsted and Vaux to the demands of the new industrial expansion. In an age that accepted social Darwinism as a rationale for social action, the survival of the fittest seemed more important than the alleviation of human distress through ecological engineering. The second was the growth in power and prestige of men of industrial wealth, for whom Olmsted worked with increasing frequency. While they generally appreciated his technical and administrative ability, and the impressive scale of his work, they usually neither shared nor fully comprehended his social and scientific goals.

There took place a corresponding shift in the way in which Olmsted perceived and defended his chief contributions to environmental planning. Where earlier he had sought to balance evenly the interests of science, social science, and art, he now conceived of planning as essentially a fine art. In part, this was a reaction to the change after 1878 from a naturalistic to a classical architecture, culminating in the World's Columbian Exposition of 1893. For Olmsted, classical architecture symbolized a decline in popular appreciation of the social and scientific substance of a natural aesthetic. However, he was compelled to participate in important projects incorporating such a classical aesthetic; hence he was intent on achieving a popular understanding of the significance of natural forms. His increasing professional involvement with projects that demanded considerable compromise brought great frustration.[4]

1. Contrasting Designs

There may, therefore, be detected in Olmsted's professional career (1857–96) two distinct periods of creativity. The first began with the prize-winning design for Central Park in 1858—"Greensward" (Figs. 2, 6, 75, 98), undertaken with the English-born and trained architect, Calvert Vaux (1824–95)—and continued through a long, politically troubled career as a professional landscape architect and Superintendent of New York City parks. This

5

public affiliation ended painfully in 1878, forcing Olmsted, in 1883, to leave New York City, the nation's most important urban center, for Brookline, Massachusetts, a suburb of Boston, where he became essentially a private practitioner. The second period may be said to have begun in 1878 and to have ended in 1893 with his landscape design for the Chicago World's Fair (Fig. 3), which took place only three years before his incapacitating terminal illness.

Placed in historic perspective, this change of environmental emphasis moved logically—even inexorably—with the major currents of American history. Olmsted's first period of achievement dovetailed precisely with three successive issues that dominated American life from 1850 until 1878—antislavery reform in the 1850's, the Civil War in the 1860's, and the effort to reconstruct the nation in the late 1860's and 1870's. The principles of freedom and equality that motivated Olmsted's opposition to slavery also prompted his environmental planning. During this time he prepared plans not only for Central Park, but also for a college at Berkeley, California (Fig. 4), for Yosemite National Park (Fig. 30), and for the community of Riverside, Illinois (Fig. 21). In addition, the financial and social success of his and Calvert Vaux's work in the cities of New York (Fig. 74) and Brooklyn (Fig. 45) and a popular belief in the public-health value of such efforts sparked the planning of parks in such cities as Chicago (Fig. 57), Buffalo (Fig. 51), Boston (Fig. 36), and Montreal (Fig. 69).

The second phase in Olmsted's design transition began some time after the failure of Reconstruction in 1877 and blossomed in the two succeeding decades, which witnessed the impact on the nation's institutions of industrialization, new immigration, accelerated economic growth, depression, and social conflict. In this period Olmsted's primarily private practice included among its principal patrons the leaders of the nation's new industrial complex. Partly to accommodate his new patrons and partly in response to altered social conditions, he developed a new design context revealed in George Vanderbilt's manorial estate, Biltmore, at Asheville, North Carolina (Fig. 29), the campus of Stanford University (Fig. 5), and the Columbian Exposition. Simultaneously, he completed designs for a park system in

6

Boston (Fig. 32) and for parks in such cities as Bridgeport, Connecticut (Fig. 44), Detroit (Fig. 61), Louisville (Figs. 15, 16, 64–68), and Rochester (Figs. 81, 82), and with his young disciple, Charles Eliot, he established the basis for regional planning in the greater Boston metropolitan area (Fig. 37).

The two major urban accomplishments that mark the start and the conclusion of Olmsted's career as an environmental planner—Central Park and the Chicago World's Fair—were prompted by two different patrons, two different sets of social conditions, and two different national and urban ideals, resulting in sharply contrasting environmental forms. While both designs reflect thoughtful and careful attention to scientific and technical matters, they are, in aesthetic and cultural terms, almost antithetical. Central Park, for the most part, is romantic in style, oriented to the land, and small-scale in detail; the Fair is classical in style, dominated by structures, and monumentally scaled. Similar contrasts can be drawn, for example, between Berkeley and Stanford (see caption to Fig. 4).

These differences are not hard-and-fast in every instance; there are, indeed, numerous design parallels in works of the two periods. In certain major project categories—notably parks—Olmsted did continue to design in a predominantly romantic—naturalistic—style. Furthermore, his work always reflected regional and local variations in climate. One of Olmsted's principal contributions to planning was the concept that shape and materials must meet the ecological requirements of a given site (Figs. 70–72, 84, 87–91, 93, 94). Therefore, he urged—early in his career—that the design of facilities for hot, arid climates resemble southern Europe more than the English precedents that influenced his own work in the East. This scientific element of his planning remained unchanged (Fig. 24). However, there was a definite shift in the general approach, reflected in some of his major efforts, and this was a direct result of the changing currents of national experience and of Olmsted's involvement in the mainstream of that history.

Both design phases of Olmsted's life, however, were joined and given creative unity by his constant search for means by which to translate humane ideals into environmental forms. Essentially, then, Olmsted's humanistic goals were not altered so much during his lifetime, nor were the planning theories and design techniques that he had continued to perfect. What shifted after 1878 was his understanding of the means—social, political, and technical—needed to effect such changes. The new center of power with respect to the environment lay with men of industrial wealth and with the designers they employed. Like his influential contemporary, Edward Bellamy, Olmsted understood the basic shift toward large-scale organization: "the tendency to wipe out small traders and concentrate business in large associations."[5] Planning, too, in order to be effective, would have to adopt a more efficient and large-scale method of organization.

A new perspective on political organization accompanied by less receptivity to the role of physical planning in alleviating social problems underlay Olmsted's basic changes in the 1880's and 90's. On the one hand, he moved to support regional planning in the Boston metropolitan area as the most effective political system of planning; on the other, the principal interpretation of his professional efforts was made in aesthetic —pure design—terms. Two events dramatize this change. For the Philadelphia Centennial Exposition of 1876 and the Paris Exposition of 1878 he exhibited a plan for the city of Buffalo (Fig. 51) that demonstrated his solutions for urban problems on many levels. For the Chicago World's Fair, he was more concerned with having landscape design included as a division of the fine arts.[6] Form rather than substance had become the principal means of defining his work to the world.

When Frederick Law Olmsted was born, America was still a predominantly agrarian nation centered on the eastern seaboard, occupying a postcolonial position as a second-rate international power. The plan for Central Park, completed a generation later, may best be understood as an expression of the idealism of a politically powerful social élite centered in the nation's economic capital, New York City. This group consisted of such formidable individuals as the newspaper editors Horace Greeley and William Cullen Bryant; Bryant's son-in-law, the journalist Parke Godwin; the Unitarian minister Henry Whitney Bellows; and the founder of the Children's Aid Society, Charles Loring Brace. They spoke

8

for powerful commercial and landed interests and were intensely conscious of the dynamic growth of cities in their lifetime. They were hopeful that the future environment of the nation could be planned to reflect the idealism of their own generation. Olmsted became their spokesman as planner.

Central Park (Figs. 2, 6, 75, 98) embodied their hope. It was a physical expression of the urban idealism contained in radical Protestant theology as expounded by the Unitarian minister William Ellery Channing and by his followers, Bellows and Bryant; in the synthetic thought of the Congregational minister Horace Bushnell and his two talented disciples, Brace and Olmsted; and in the writings of the French Utopian Socialist Charles Fourier and two of his most devoted followers, Horace Greeley and Parke Godwin. Even the generally antiurban philosophy of Ralph Waldo Emerson provided intellectual sustenance for environmental reformers by emphasizing nature and natural forms.[7]

The public park was one of those rare institutions embodying the spirit of a society: its utopian goals, specific social needs, and form of expression. Those influenced by Fourier could see the public park as the center of a new community; followers of Channing and Bushnell had been educated to understand the importance of open spaces to the poor living in squalid tenements; liberal Christians believed, too, in the power of recreation to modify antisocial behavior; and Transcendentalists could identify with the spiritual value of secular institutions cast in natural forms. All could accept the park as a unifying institution: a catalyst in the creation of a homogeneous democratic culture.

By 1855 followers of these interrelated ideals had accepted the city as the arena of activity. More importantly, they understood that the future of the nation—rural or urban—would depend upon the vitality of the city. For this group, one of the nation's chief resources was the creative capacity of its people—and creativity, they understood, was an urban product. If American cities, they reasoned, could not respond innovatively to society's many problems, what hope was there for the rest of the nation? Thus, they were advocates of environmental planning, denouncing as primitive and barbaric all opposition to such planning. With a unanimity rare among intellectuals, they were convinced that the greatest threat to the nation's social future was not the city, as difficult as its many problems were even in 1855, but rather the vast, formless, sparsely settled frontier, which they regarded as violent, atavistic, and inherently thoughtless.[8]

By the time of Olmsted's death on August 28, 1903, America had been transformed—almost completely—into an urban-centered nation (Figs. 33–35) covering an entire continent and occupying an international position as a world power. But few of the hopes of an earlier generation for the development of a truly humane urban civilization had been fulfilled. Indeed, in many respects, the nation seemed more divided along economic and social lines than it had been fifty years before, and Olmsted's social and intellectual élite had been displaced from the position of economic, social, and political power it had held at the time of the Civil War. With that displacement was submerged —but not extinguished—the concept of environmental planning evidenced in the design of Central Park. The rejection of scientific and humane planning characterized by the frontier had for the most part conquered the city.

The post-Civil War period had brought into being a new set of social conditions magnifying old problems to fearsome proportions. The architecture of the World's Columbian Exposition, revealed to the public in 1893, incorporated a new idealism best expressed in Edward Bellamy's utopian novel *Looking Backward.* It was an idealism similar in social goals and spirit to the philosophy expressed in 1855, but distinctly different in process and form. Bellamy's utopian society, vastly more centralized and organized than the communitarian concept reflected in the thought of an earlier period, was welcomed by Olmsted's aging generation of reformers, concentrated in the city of Boston.[9] Their acceptance of such a solution was in part a measure of the postwar failure to create a satisfying national culture, the goal of Olmsted's earlier theories and techniques of environmental planning.

10

2. An Aristocratic Designer: Richard Morris Hunt

This basic transformation in Olmsted's design solutions is also evidenced in his increasing collaboration with Richard Morris Hunt (1825–95), whose commission to design the Administration Building, a showpiece of the Columbian Exposition, merely capped a long, unbroken career as America's most fashionable architect. In sharp contrast to Olmsted and the architect co-designer of Central Park, Calvert Vaux, Hunt had no difficulty in accommodating his style of architecture to the new sources of power and wealth in post-Civil War America. His principal professional interest remained, as one contemporary recalled, "decorating the . . . privacies of the Vanderbilts and Goelets, the Marquands and Astors, the Belmonts and . . . Gerrys."[10]

Hunt was the first American graduate of the École des Beaux Arts in Paris. He was there during the reconstruction of Paris under Napoleon III, in which endeavor he assisted in 1854 with the additions to the Louvre and the Tuileries.[11] He was quick to sense the affinity that American millionaires had for French aristocratic splendor. Hunt provided his clients with an imaginative rendering of what they admired. Aristocratic power was the pervasive theme of the châteaulike mansions he constructed on New York City's Fifth Avenue, the most important boundary of Central Park. He offered a similar design in 1864 to The New-York Historical Society, which was then contemplating locating in Central Park on the present site of the Armory. "When our friend Hunt," wrote Olmsted, "brought forward a plan for a building of the Historical Society last winter, one of the Committee on Architecture described [it] to me by saying 'You would not know it from the Louvre.' "[12]

It was logical to expect, therefore, that when the opportunity arose, Hunt would attempt to alter the design of the park itself, which was the social and design antithesis of the monumental architecture that he envisioned for Fifth Avenue. Hunt's chance came in 1863—after both Olmsted and Vaux had resigned from their positions with the Central Park project—when the Board of Commissioners advertised for plans to complete the construction of the gateways and the approaches to the park. Hunt was awarded the commission in 1864, but his designs were not made public until the late spring of 1865, when they were prominently displayed in the new building of the National Academy of Design. The plans, accompanied by an explanatory text, were then published.

The suggested changes were drastic. Although Hunt presented plans for only four of the entrances to the park, these were the principal approaches along Fifty-ninth Street—corner of Fifth Avenue, opposite Sixth Avenue, opposite Seventh Avenue, and corner of Eighth Avenue. In addition, it was expected that Hunt would design about twenty more gates and approaches. He proposed an aristocratic facade to the park, including monumental, imperial-styled gates, formal plazas leading to the main entranceways, and a more symmetrical design than Olmsted and Vaux's for the roads and paths leading from the main gates (Figs. 7, 8).

The contrast with the Greensward plan was dramatic. Instead of following a design that set the park apart from Fifth Avenue, Hunt proposed that it become an appendage to that street of wealth and power. In Olmsted and Vaux's design there were no gates, no plazas leading to the main entrances; instead, informal, winding paths led from the entranceway. In defense of Hunt's proposal, an anonymous author—possibly the architect himself—explained the social basis of the new design. "It is folly," he wrote,

> . . . to attempt rural entrances for a park in the heart of a great city, surrounded by magnificent edifices of fashion, as our Central Park will soon be. . . . The entrances should be in keeping with the future external surroundings of the Park, and establish the connection between the street architecture without and cultivated nature within.[13]

The public disclosure of these plans and the debate that they stimulated only seemed to muddle the principles motivating each design. "The style in which Hunt's plans have been publicly discussed," Olmsted wrote, "in most cases hitherto has been very distasteful to me." Vaux responded to the substitute plans with more detailed criticism. As a trained architect, which Olmsted was not, he was particularly anxious that the principles behind their original design be clearly fixed in the public mind. Therefore, he urged a prominent architectural critic, Clarence Cook, his and Olmsted's friend, to issue "a line by line" refutation of Hunt's plans.[14]

The point to be stressed was that Hunt's revision would have altered the social significance of the design—transforming a democratic into an aristocratic aesthetic. "The park," Vaux wrote, "is what we have been fighting for and the gates typify what we have been fighting against—it is Nap[oleon] III in disguise all over." In the urban ideal held by the supporters of the Greensward plan, a park would need "to have no gates—to keep open house and trust always." In addition, Hunt's proposal—substituting man-made materials for natural ones—would have radically altered the passerby's perception of the park. It was the view of the landscape, Vaux asserted, that was "everything—[and] the architecture—nothing." The heart of the original design was to translate "democratic ideas into trees and dirt."[15] The defeat of Hunt's plans was merely another indication of the power and support that was still Olmsted's in 1865.

Yet by 1888 Olmsted would collaborate with Hunt on George C. Vanderbilt's estate, "Biltmore," at Asheville, North Carolina (Fig. 29). Cooperation took place notwithstanding Hunt's grandiose design for the main building and Olmsted's opposition to many of Hunt's wishes. As Gifford Pinchot, the pioneer scientific forester, recalled,

> Biltmore House . . . was a magnificent chateau of Indiana limestone. With the terrace and stables, it was a thousand feet in length. Its setting was superb, the view from it breath-taking, and as a feudal castle it would have been beyond criticism, and perhaps beyond praise.
>
> But in the United States of the nineteenth century and among the one-room cabins of the Appalachian mountaineers, it did not belong. The contrast was a devastating commentary on the injustice of concentrated wealth.[16]

13

Two years later, Olmsted assumed responsibility for the site plan of the World's Columbian Exposition, in which Hunt's Administration Building echoed the dominant monumental motif of the Fair and of its leader, the architect-planner-manager Daniel Burnham. Olmsted's cooperation with Hunt and Burnham is understandable in the perspective of a new historical condition. He was compelled to accept the reality that the nation had produced a large class of men of wealth whose demands for large-scale planning and design would constitute an ever-increasing aspect of his work. Biltmore was not just another large private project. As Olmsted explained to his business partners, he could not "help being influenced by the great numbers of rich and commanding men that cross our roads on their way to all parts of the North, and whose impressions are to affect our future business."[17]

Indeed, Hunt and Burnham always had known where economic power lay and how to attach themselves to it. The Columbian Exposition incorporated many social and cultural values, and it reflected a new power of planners interested in comprehensive design. But it was power that depended more on new wealth than on the popular support of socially concerned journalists, ministers, social workers, and artists, which Olmsted and Vaux had enjoyed in 1857, when Central Park was being planned.

Central Park was more than an isolated design. As Olmsted explained it to Parke Godwin, the park was "a democratic development of the highest significance and on the success of which, in my opinion, much of the progress of art and aesthetic culture in this country is dependent."[18] As the antithesis of the sparsely settled, uncivilized frontier that he had encountered in the "slave states" of the South and in the American West, it represented a totally new environment reflecting international influence, social and scientific theories, and the abundance of design talent available in a large urban area.

3. A Democratic Planner: Frederick Law Olmsted

Olmsted's conception of physical form as a function of social planning was perhaps his most important contribution. He was a social critic and theorist before becoming a professional planner and designer. Olmsted was thirty-five when he began work on Central Park. And it was not until after the Civil War, when he was more than forty, that his career as a landscape architect was clearly determined. His personal quest for fulfillment was always characterized by immersion in some endeavor to which he devoted himself completely so long as he deemed it to be in the best interest of the nation. That is, his works were responsive to social needs and were drawn from a variety of intellectual disciplines.

For much of the period before 1850, Olmsted pursued a career in farming. The establishment of model farms of scientific agriculture and management seemed to him to be in the national interest. In this effort Olmsted was conforming to the philosophy of Thomas Jefferson and of Andrew Jackson Downing, America's foremost land-use theorist during the second quarter of the nineteenth century. On a personal level, scientific agriculture presented a challenge that marshaled all of his interests and talents. "Rural pursuits," he wrote to his brother, ". . . tend to elevate and enlarge the ideas, for all the proudest aims of Science are involved in them. . . . I believe that our farmers are, and have cause to be, the most contented men in the world."[19]

There is no simple explanation for Olmsted's transition from scientific farmer to environmental planner and designer. It is sufficient to note that one occupation replaced the other as all-absorbing and was viewed in precisely the same social frame of reference. The inner man was somehow fulfilled in the challenge of Central Park. "If a fairy had shaped it for me," Olmsted confessed, "it could not have fitted me better. It was normal, ordinary and naturally outgrowing from my previous life . . . and it occupied my whole heart."[20]

However, Olmsted could not have found this depth of personal satisfaction had he not already perceived the planning and design of a park in terms of social and cultural issues. Such a perspective was made possible by four experiences that took place between 1850 and 1857; each of these experiences was related to a larger issue of national concern. The first was Olmsted's move to Staten Island in 1848, where he owned and operated a scientific farm. He quickly became part of the social and literary élite of New York, the nation's "capital" city. In addition, he adopted the basic tenets of Utopian Socialism held in whole or in part by some of his closest friends, such as Parke Godwin. This group endeavored to improve the city through public institutions such as schools, parks, hospitals, and museums.

The second experience was Olmsted's walking tour through the British Isles and western Europe in search of an understanding of European civilization. Although the principal purpose of the trip was to report on agricultural matters, it is quite clear from the book Olmsted published and from the record of that trip left by his traveling companion and childhood friend, Charles Loring Brace, that they had immersed themselves in a whole range of environmental and social matters. Most significant was Olmsted's awareness that such critical problems as urbanization, poverty, crime, and prostitution were international in scope. Environmental planning and design was an international issue, and Olmsted, like Brace, had profited from the various reform experiments being pioneered abroad.[21]

The third experience was the antislavery crusade, gaining force in the 1850's. In part because of the favorable reception to his book, *Walks and Talks of an American Farmer,* Olmsted was invited by Henry Raymond, editor of *The New York Times,* to undertake a series of tours through the South for the purpose of presenting an objective description of the effect of slavery on physical and social conditions there. This he did, and in the process wrote three long books on the subject that were considered—then as now—outstanding descriptions of southern life. Just as crucial to Olmsted, however, was the way in which he now perceived social issues. The trips and the writing, in conjunction with the heightening of sectional tensions in 1854–55, led Olmsted to view the nation as polarized between two societies, the chief cause of these tensions being the environmental and social deficiencies of the South brought about by slavery. The need for an improved policy of planning was elevated to a new level of national priority.[22]

Finally, in 1855, Olmsted became part-owner and an editor of *Putnam's Monthly Magazine,* an avant-garde intellectual periodical concerned with social, political, scientific, and aesthetic matters. *Putnam's* became a national forum for the most advanced liberal thought. Olmsted was in a position to commission articles on a whole range of matters related to the future of the nation.[23]

These four experiences made it possible for him to transfer his interest in scientific agriculture to other matters. Furthermore, he was able to view the public park as a prototypical form for an improved urban environment—an example, as it were, of northern civilization as opposed to southern decadence. But before becoming a committed professional landscape architect, Olmsted had two other formative experiences. The first was his direct involvement in the Civil War (1861–63) as Executive Secretary of the United States Sanitary Commission (which was to become the American Red Cross). This essentially private organization commanded the services of most of the nation's leading scientists. It became, under Olmsted's leadership, the most comprehensive effort in the nation's history to research, plan, and coordinate policies and programs affecting the daily life of the soldier. The Commission was concerned with such aspects of military life as physical facilities, diet, and medicine. In addition, Olmsted viewed the army as a basis for measuring the effects of national social conditions on the general population.[24]

Olmsted left the Commission in 1863 for the world of private industry. He assumed the directorship of the Mariposa Mining Estates in California, a vast gold-mining enterprise controlled by eastern interests. During his period as manager, Olmsted viewed the enterprise as a challenge to comprehensive planning. He was as interested in the homes of the miners and in making available to them such facilities as reading rooms and coffee houses as he was in the management and design of the physical plant. The two, in his view, were interrelated.[25]

By 1865, when he returned to New York City from California, Olmsted had developed a set of social and physical principles on environmental planning, design, and management. Some of these principles would shift as to order of priority or would be reinterpreted to meet new social conditions, but in no instance were they consciously violated or discarded during his long, varied, and politically troubled career as a planner, designer, and manager. Nevertheless, he was compelled to alter his means of expression and the form of his work.

II
SOCIAL AND PHYSICAL PRINCIPLES

1. Social Architecture

Although never used by Olmsted as such, the term "social architecture" remains the closest description of what he was attempting. The phrase was first used by Parke Godwin to describe the importance placed by American followers of Charles Fourier on the need for new communities.[26] Godwin and Olmsted sought to adapt Utopian Socialism to American conditions and to a Jeffersonian tradition of democracy. In the view of Olmsted and his coterie, America, because of its unique position as the world's youngest and most dynamic democracy, was called upon to demonstrate in physical terms innovative responses to the social problems of an industrializing and urbanizing nation. The nation had to prove that a democracy organized in the eighteenth century to meet the needs of a rural population could still retain the basic elements of a Jeffersonian ideology within the new forms required for urban living.

Jefferson's influence was dominant in American intellectual circles, in spite of his essentially antiurban judgments, expressed in *Notes on the State of Virginia.* Olmsted's friend, the prominent Unitarian minister Henry Whitney Bellows, singled out these passages for critical discussion.[27] Yet Bellows—like Olmsted and others—in his writings and work adhered to Jefferson's guiding principle: America must fulfill a particular democratic destiny unlike that of any European nation. Social progress in a democracy could not be measured—as among aristocratic nations—by the advancement of any single class or group of individuals. It had to be widespread. The final mark of a democracy would be made "among those classes which form the majority of the people of a country . . . [among whom] should be found the best evidence of the wisdom of national institutions."[28]

The essential aspiration of Olmsted's group—like that of Jefferson's—was for America to develop a distinctively superior, yet homogeneous and harmonious, civilization to serve as an example for the divided and warring continent of Europe. "With us," wrote Charles Brace, "there is not this past history of intense jealousy and unceasing dissension, there is not the local boundary, which at once separated religions and interests." Providence, Parke Godwin believed, had designated "this continent, and the people, for a homogeneous civilization." And Horace Bushnell, quoting the poet Milton, believed that America should become "as one Christian personage, one mighty growth and stature of an honest man, as big and compact in virtue as in body."[29]

Such emphasis on national unity and homogeneity of culture was—at least in part—a reaction to the repeated doubts and fears expressed by such foreign commentators as De Tocqueville, Dickens, and Macauley, who felt that, given the varied social elements in American society, no consensus could be achieved within a democratic system of representative government. This concern became more pronounced with the extraordinary immigration of Irish and German Catholics into America's major cities during the period 1830–50. By 1855, for example, the foreign-born composed 52 percent of New York City's inhabitants. The immigrant proportion of the working class of that city was even higher—about 70 percent. To those who, like Olmsted, were guided by social statistics, it was clear, even before the Civil War, that any presumed national homogeneity or unity was gone. "Taking the people of the United States altogether," Olmsted wrote, "the majority are by no means of Anglo-Saxon origin."[30]

This process of social change accelerated during the post-Civil War period. Industrialization continued to narrow the economic base of rural life—Jefferson's hope for the future—and to make the nation more dependent on the city. During his travels through the nation in the 1850's and '60's, Olmsted saw what seemed to him to be the disappearance of an older, Jeffersonian way of life—

> the meeting-house closed, the church dilapidated; the famous old taverns, stores, mills, and offices dropping to pieces and vacant, or perhaps with a mere corner occupied by day laborers; but a third as many children as formerly . . . in the school-houses, and of these less than half of American-born parents.[31]

2. The Challenge of the City

The second basic assumption that underscored Olmsted's work was the need to understand and accept the total dimensions of the urban revolution. He was troubled by the pervasive nature of this process. A democracy originating in rural America—proclaimed by many to be a utopian form of society—would have to adapt itself to the city. "Our country has entered upon a stage of progress," he wrote, "in which its welfare is to depend on the convenience, safety, order and economy of life in its great cities. It . . . cannot gain in virtue, wisdom, comfort, except as they also advance."[32] The metropolis, he predicted, would become the typical setting of American life.

While Olmsted accepted as inevitable the growth of cities, he was concerned that the life-style of the town or village community was disappearing. In small communities, he recalled,

20

families, however self-contained, were responsive to the needs of others. They were independent and contented, and neighborliness and kindness seemed to come naturally within such environments. Olmsted, like the planners of utopian communities, wanted to preserve this social atmosphere. In later life, noting the changes that had come to some of the New England villages —the railroad, the summer crowds, the new villas and roads—he lamented that none of them made the village appear "as beautiful" as the original scene of his childhood. The solution to this problem lay in study, analysis, planning, and design in anticipation of the continuing process of urbanization. He studied census reports and other data pertaining to internal migration. Each of his planning reports on American cities published in the nineteenth century was based on this kind of analysis.[33]

Olmsted presented a theory of urbanization as fixed and immutable as any "iron-law" of nature. He pointed out that the character of social and industrial life compelled a functional separation of work and home, which in turn demanded a physical division between places of work and residence. Businessmen no longer needed to dwell where they worked. "In the last century," Olmsted wrote,

> comparatively few towns-people occupied dwellings distinctly separate from their place of business. A large majority of the citizens of Paris, London and of New York do so to-day, and the tendency to divisions of the town corresponding to this change of habits must rapidly increase with their further enlargement, because of the greater distance which will exist between their different parts.[34]

This physical separation was based on the changing needs of society. Olmsted described the schism according to the categories "commercial" and "domestic." At work, he wrote, men of affairs increasingly demanded concentration of services and buildings, and reduction of time spent in business:

> The necessity of personal conference in regard to affairs requiring separate offices, gives increasing value to time during certain hours, and distance is for these purposes yet

equivalent in the market to time. Hence vicinity to various offices becomes an increasing element of value.

The increasing specialization in business, which often makes many sources of supply necessary to be called on for a purpose which could formerly be served by one, tends in the same general direction; the result being always an increasing motive to compactness.[35]

The outstanding urban symbol of this change was the emerging high-rise building. Olmsted was acquainted with the architects principally responsible for this fundamental innovation. "At every center of commerce," he wrote, ". . . more and more business tends to come under each roof, and, in the progress of building, walls are carried higher and higher, and deeper and deeper, so that now 'vertical railways' are coming in vogue."[36]

Workers in the dense and confined inner city sought relief and escape from the physical environment of a more demanding and concentrated workday. "The reason is obvious," Olmsted wrote:

> . . . when not engaged in business, [the worker] has no occasion to be near his working place, but demands arrangements of a wholly different character. Families require to settle in certain localities in sufficient numbers to support those establishments which minister to their social and other wants, and yet are not willing to accept the conditions of town-life which were formerly deemed imperative, and which, in the business quarters, are yet, perhaps, in some degree, imperative, but demand as much of the luxuries of free air, space and abundant vegetation as, without loss of town-privileges, they can be enabled to secure.[37]

These requirements were to be met by the suburb (Figs. 21, 22, 73, 78).

22

3. An Organic Society

The image of an organic whole remained constant in Olmsted's planning and design theory. His work was the formal expression of a belief in a self-regulating society. In this scheme of things, planners would address themselves to social needs and physical functions unfulfilled by the forces of the marketplace. Olmsted tended toward a classical economic view of society. Throughout his career he remained opposed to monopolies, whether of business or labor. Similarly, he rejected and fought against political influence in matters of professional concern, for such intervention, in his opinion, drove the cost of civic projects to astronomical heights and the quality to abysmal depths.

Such beliefs led to an untold number of conflicts with established organizations. Olmsted was adamant in condemning the efforts of businessmen to appropriate those scarce resources that ought to belong to all the people (Fig. 80). He was equally opposed to—and fought—the efforts of organized labor to obtain wages that he considered excessive, and he resisted political bosses who sought to place unqualified workers on the public payroll. In the tradition of the classical economists, he held that the freedom of the marketplace was in the public interest and most likely to lead to higher quality.[38]

Such freedom, however, had to be directed toward realizing social ideals unfulfilled in American society. It did not, and could not, signify antagonism toward social or physical planning. The processes of industrialization and urbanization, if allowed to proceed without planning, would permanently undermine individual freedom. Like the Utopian Socialists, Olmsted was alarmed at the incidence of "social failures" visible in urban centers. The increase in the number of criminals, of the mentally ill, of alcoholics, of prostitutes, and of poor people concentrated in cities was as much an index of the state of that society's health as were its successful numbers. Moreover, as he and all of the social theorists of his age understood, the relationship between the two classes—those who failed and those who succeeded— was constant. They were both wedded, as it were, to the place and time in which they lived, locked together by the same social forces.[39]

A goal of society, Olmsted approvingly quoted the French Socialist activist Louis Blanc, was "to restore to the dignity of human nature those whom the excess of poverty degrades."[40] A democratic society must seek to eradicate or alleviate those social ills for which the system itself was partially or wholly responsible. Freedom must be balanced by equality. The two ideals, in fact—freedom and equality—created the tension within the democratic ethos that led to constructive conflict. Moreover, no people could be creative—or endure—if equal opportunity were not provided for satisfying such basic needs as education, recreation, and a healthy and pleasant environment.

The key to maintaining a viable society, Olmsted emphasized, was the development of leaders capable of gathering and analyzing social data and formulating public policy. Such leadership, he wrote in a Jeffersonian context, would display "that form of conscientiousness that attends the honorable possession of honorable advantages"—a commitment to the well-being of the community and the nation.[41]

By the time Olmsted offered this description, he recognized that ordinary politicians would not provide this kind of leadership; he viewed most elected officials, especially in local government, as self-serving, if not downright corrupt, and lacking in any perspective larger than the immediate. Statesmen could not be elected—they had to be nurtured as much as any plant or tree. In his judgment, for instance, such men and women had come forth to serve in the United States Sanitary Commission during the Civil War; to perpetuate this leadership and to further these ideals, Olmsted assisted in the founding of the Union League Club of New York City and the periodical *The Nation.*

4. Education and Recreation

To foster such a "natural" leadership, Olmsted laid great emphasis, as had Jefferson, on a comprehensive, integrated system of education. Except for homes and communities, there was no

24

other institution so critical to the future of a democracy. To advance social and cultural growth, it was essential that the average citizen "reads similar books, wears similar clothing, has similar amusements, and dwells in a similar house, with similar furniture" to that of the more privileged.[42]

Olmsted was interested in all stages of education—from the preschool years to the university. He was impressed with the nursery schools for children of working-class mothers that he had seen in Amsterdam, in which, he had noted, "there was no crying and fretting," and with the fact that among the infants in plantation nurseries—overseen by slaves—"not a baby of them [seemed irritable]." The nursery school, he concluded in the 1850's, had a role in the formation of personality. His experiences demonstrated "how young the little twig is bent, how early the formation of habits commences."[43]

Olmsted's principal educational focus was, however, the university, the final training ground for democratic leadership. He believed, like Jefferson, that higher education should be part of a continuous and interrelated educational system transmitting shared values of the highest standard. "It seems to me," he wrote to his friend, Charles Eliot Norton, whose Cambridge, Massachusetts, estate Olmsted was planning to integrate into the Harvard campus, "extremely desirable that in some way Alma Mater should be the mother common to all classes, though some go out from her into the world only a year old, others two, others five, others six, and some remain, as fellows, much longer periods."[44]

But Olmsted's concept of education was not limited to the written or spoken word. Indeed, he doubted that the most influential aspect of the educative process took place within the classroom. "San Francisco," he wrote, "boasts of her schoolhouses, but the most important part of education is not that given by the schoolmaster." The character of the child was "more influenced," he believed, "by conditions out of school than conditions in school." This distinction was an important one, for Olmsted was extending the traditional meaning of democratic education to include all of the planned environment. Hence the responsibility of democratic governments for education encompassed more than the provision of buildings, books, and teachers.[45]

To Olmsted, as to the philosophical leaders of his generation —Emerson and Bushnell—education was not a set of formalized experiences limited to the young and taking place within some specific structure. It was the total process of life in which every human being was engaged every second. For this Transcendental-minded group, the impact of the environment on the senses was critical. The increasing tempo of life, particularly evident in cities, mandated alternative environments that were tranquil for what Olmsted termed "passive recreation" (Figs. 6, 15, 16). It was a democratic obligation to provide such public facilities, for no individual could or would make available the necessary land. It was in the public spaces—parks, streets, campuses, and hospital grounds—that citizens would experience the reality of democratic life.

But provision for passive recreation was not sufficient. The unity of work and life had been so disrupted that urbanites required increased facilities for active recreation as well (Figs. 17, 18, 99–101, 104, 105). Olmsted condemned the "Poor Richard" ideal of life in which only work was glorified. He felt that the failure to provide spaces for active recreation and to encourage leisure activities was a serious national defect. He urged that young and old alike be shown that play was a requirement "of healthful, virtuous and respectable life equally important with any other." And he deplored the fact that in the 1870's "compared with any other civilized nation the poverty of our cities . . . is very marked . . . in respect to means, facilities and encouragement to healthful and enriching recreation."[46]

A system of recreation managed as part of a city's educational resources was, in his opinion, necessary to an organic society. Without such facilities, individual creativity and productivity would be seriously hampered. "Since all wealth," Olmsted wrote,

> is the result of labor, and every man's individual wealth is, on the whole, increased by the labor of every other in the community, . . . it follows that, without recuperation and recreation . . . the power of each individual to labor wisely and

26

honestly is soon lost, and that, without . . . recuperation . . . the power of each individual to add to the wealth of the community is, as a necessary consequence, also soon lost.[47]

5. A National Perspective

The fact that Olmsted's projects are still extant in every section of the country and in many American cities is not only a matter of chance or merely evidence of an increasingly successful professional practice. It was as much a reflection of his concern for the entire nation at a time of rapid development. Environmental challenges were not restricted to any one region. By the 1880's Olmsted was regarded at home and abroad as the nation's principal environmental planner. "In all my wide travel over this country," a leading educator wrote him, "from Portland, Oregon, to Portland, Maine, I never see any mark of woodland or landscape taste and training that I do not refer to your labors."[48]

The creative designer had to be involved with a range of plans —not simply with one category or one set of clients. Olmsted is best remembered for the design of his large urban parks, such as Central Park in New York City, South Park (now Washington and Jackson parks) in Chicago (Fig. 58), Belle Isle Park in Detroit (Fig. 63), Franklin Park in Boston (Fig. 42), and Seneca Park in Rochester. But he participated as well in the planning and design of many other projects, including individual residences (Figs. 9–11, 13), public buildings (Figs. 12, 26, 85, 86), mental hospitals (Fig. 25), railway stations (Fig. 14), cemeteries (Fig. 24), campuses (Figs. 4, 5, 23), residential communities (Figs. 21, 22, 73), and "national" parks (Figs. 30, 31).

This comprehensive point of view regarding planning bound Olmsted for long periods to two architects in particular—Calvert Vaux and Henry Hobson Richardson. With Vaux, Olmsted designed Central Park in New York City, Prospect Park in Brooklyn (Fig. 46), and many of the smaller parks and squares (Figs. 47, 48), in those cities. In addition, as partners in private practice, Olmsted and Vaux worked on the plans for the University of California at Berkeley and for the community of Riverside,

Illinois. In addition, they collaborated on the restoration and preservation of the American Falls at Niagara as part of an international project. With Richardson, Olmsted worked on private residences, railway stations for the Albany and Boston Railroad, the Buffalo State Hospital (for the mentally ill), North Easton Town Hall, the Albany State Capitol, and a "master-plan" for Staten Island, New York.[49]

6. A Cooperative Design Process

Effective cooperation among practitioners of different professions on so varied a range of tasks could take place because these men shared similar views regarding the *process of design.* They accepted the principle that a design was the end result of an analytical, problem-solving process—a meaningful solution rather than an isolated decoration. Design problems originated in the ecology (Figs. 20, 27, 62, 73) and the proposed uses of the site (Figs. 78, 98). The designer's tools were the available technology (Figs. 90–97) and his own creative imagination. Economic and technical considerations were subordinated to ecological, social, and aesthetic needs.

This principle of scientific design was really an adaptation of the theories and methods of scientific farming. Olmsted and his associates believed that the method of analyzing data that resulted in healthful conditions for plants and animals would be equally rewarding in planning for humans. The concept of the ideal garden or forest was an equally desirable environmental goal for people.

Although the term "ecology" was not widely used in Olmsted's age, it is quite clear that this frame of reference shaped his work. For at least until Robert Koch's demonstration of the cholera vibrio in 1883, environmental planning was highly conditioned and mandated by the primitive fear of death from epidemic diseases that periodically paralyzed all major cities. In the absence of a well-defined concept of "germs" and "viruses," physicians as well as other scientists looked to environmental

28

conditions to explain the causes of death and disease[50] (Figs. 39, 84).

The social implications of ecology were apparent. In a century that saw the birth of sociology as well as other social sciences, it was logical to believe that scientific analysis of society could lead to an amelioration of social ills. Indeed, the considerable literature of this period on crime, alcoholism, poverty, and mental illness placed great emphasis on environmental cures. Slums were studied increasingly as diseased urban tissue, suffering, among other things, from deficiencies in pure air and water, sunlight, and open space.

As a corollary to this principle, it was accepted that any large project required a team effort consisting of such specialists as a civil engineer, an agricultural engineer, and a horticulturist, in addition to an architect and a landscape architect. This integrated approach to environmental planning was basic to the success of Olmsted's first major project, Central Park, and to all subsequent ones. Much of the technical success of Central Park was owing to Olmsted's ability to attract co-workers of very high technical competence.

Each of these men was to become a recognized leader in his field. George Waring, Jr., who was responsible for drainage, went on to become a pioneer in urban sanitary engineering (Fig. 94); William Grant, the civil engineer responsible for road design and construction, made important theoretical contributions to this phase of engineering (Figs. 90–93). The selection, adaptation, and maintenance of natural materials—plants, shrubs, and trees—and their planting design was the contribution of Ignaz Pilat, a European-born and educated horticulturist; the design of all physical structures in the park—bridges, houses, monuments, and walls—was the responsibility of Calvert Vaux (Figs. 99–103); the overall concept of the urban public park–its functions and design–was Olmsted and Vaux's. But the supervision of this team effort and the continued maintenance of the park (Figs. 95–97) was clearly the responsibility of the landscape architect.[51]

III

ENVIRONMENTAL PLANNING AND DESIGN

1. Urban Open Spaces

Olmsted's contributions to the planning of cities spanned almost forty years. During this time he designed many kinds of open spaces in various areas of the country. While the functions of these spaces often overlapped, at least eight different types can be distinguished: **1.** large "country" parks planned to serve a variety of recreational activities for the entire city, but which are not part of a physically interrelated park system, such as Mount Royal in Montreal (Fig. 70); Belle Isle in Detroit (Fig. 63); and Beardsley Park in Bridgeport (Fig. 44); **2.** large multi-use open rural-type spaces planned and designed as part of a physically interconnected municipal park system, such as Prospect Park, Brooklyn (Fig. 46); Delaware Park, Buffalo (Fig. 52); Cherokee Park, Louisville (Fig. 65); and Franklin Park, Boston (Fig. 42); **3.** heavily wooded areas within urban boundaries planned as much as examples of conservation as for recreational use, such

30

as Lynn Woods, Lynn, Massachusetts (Fig. 20); and Iroquois Park, Louisville (Fig. 64); **4.** the parkway, boulevard, and riverway, which, in addition to serving as physical links between parks and communities, were designed as linear open spaces, such as Eastern Parkway in Brooklyn (Fig. 50) and the parkway system in Buffalo (Fig. 51); **5.** more localized open spaces designed to serve particular neighborhoods or areas of a city, such as Fort Greene Park, Brooklyn (Fig. 48); the South Park System, Chicago (Fig. 58); the Front (Fig. 53) and South Park in Buffalo (Fig. 56); Wood Island Park, Boston (Fig. 43); and Riverside Park (Fig. 77) and Morningside Park (Fig. 79) in New York City; **6.** more specialized open spaces, such as Tompkins Park, Brooklyn (Fig. 49); Logan Place, Louisville (**Figs. 15, 16**); Niagara Square, Buffalo (Fig. 55); the Back Bay (Figs. 38, 39); the Jamaica Pond (Fig. 40); and the Arnold Arboretum (Fig. 41) in Boston; the Parade Ground in Brooklyn (Fig. 47) and The Parade, in Buffalo (Fig. 54); beaches such as Marine Park, Boston (Fig. 18); riverside parks such as Seneca Park, Rochester (Fig. 82), and a plan for Pawtucket, Rhode Island (Fig. 80); urban-centered fairs such as the Columbian Exposition (Fig. 3); burial places such as Mountain View Cemetery, Oakland, California (Fig. 24); zoological gardens such as that for Central Park, New York City (Fig. 19); and playgrounds such as Charlesbank, in Boston (Fig. 17), and Boone Square, in Louisville, Kentucky (Fig. 67); **7.** the siting of public buildings oriented as much to the view of the structure as to the use of the surrounding grounds, such as North Easton Town Hall (Fig. 12); the Buffalo State Hospital (Fig. 25); the United States Capitol, Washington, D.C. (Figs. 85, 86); and the Boston and Albany Railroad stations (Fig. 14); **8.** and, finally, Olmsted was equally concerned with the siting of homes, organized principally for functional family use and the perception of the user, such as the Robert Treat Paine house, Waltham, Massachusetts (Figs. 9–11). In each case, his design was based on his evolving understanding of the needs of persons living in cities and of the responsibility of planners to their clients.[52]

2. Planned Communities: Suburbs

A plan proposed by Olmsted and Vaux to link the city of Newark, New Jersey, by parkway with Llewellyn Park, America's first planned romantic suburb, is significant on two levels.[53] First, it reflects Olmsted's and Vaux's regard for that achievement, which served as a prototype for all their future efforts to plan communities; second, it emphasizes the fact that the parkway was more than merely an alternative to the ordinary city street. It was designed also as a route to a specific place: the planned community. Considering the importance of planned communities to Olmsted's social theory, it is sad to note that he had so few opportunities to design them. It soon became clear that the publicly financed parks and parkways, which Olmsted hoped would lead to cooperatively—but privately—financed communities, were not inspiring such efforts on any large scale. Parks and parkways generated the development of handsome architecture on their tree-lined borders, but rarely produced any systematized and communally oriented use of surrounding land. Urban land remained under the control of the speculative land developer.

The concept of the planned community, as executed in Llewellyn Park and in Olmsted's adaptation of that form, was quite revolutionary in American urban development.[54] It is true, of course, that planned communities developed by religious groups were part of the American experience. The planned secular community was the successor to such religiously and Utopian-based communities as Oneida, Brook Farm, and Red Bank. What was radically different in Llewellyn Park and in Olmsted's work was the concept of the planned secular community that would not polarize city and country. It was as different in social orientation and physical form from the typical real-estate subdivision as the concept of a public park and parkway was from the traditional urban environment.

Public parks were meant to be a countervailing force in the essentially commercial city, improving the urban environment; the planned suburb was a part of the city in the countryside. All of the care taken to design the public park according to the social needs of the users and the physical demands of a given site was now to be applied to the planned community. More-over, the nation required planned suburban development to promote a healthy urban environment and to protect the countryside. "Spread city" was ultimately destructive, socially and physically, to all environmental forms.

The suburb, as Olmsted conceived of it, was not intended to be (as suburbs now generally are) far removed from the heart of the city. The goal—recurrent in present-day planning literature —was to develop communities within easy reach of the city center, inhabited by "urban villagers." Olmsted believed that new methods of improving roads (Figs. 91, 93), the many varieties of the light carriage (which had come into use in the nineteenth century), and the steam car—of which there were more than 400 in use on common roads by 1870—would facilitate rapid transportation between home and work.[55]

There was, he felt, no technical reason why the suburb should not combine the best features of city and country. The cultural advantages of urban life, he realized, would be lost to "people living in houses a quarter or a half a mile apart." Yet urban life need not be synonymous with "an unhealthy density of population." In fact, the advantages of civilization were best realized in "suburban neighborhoods where each family abode stands fifty or a hundred feet or more apart from all others, and at some distance from the public road." Good roads and walks, adequate sewerage, a pure water supply, gas to light the dark streets, and low-cost, rapid, and comfortable transportation to urban centers could, he believed, "give any farming land in a healthy and attractive situation the value of town lots."[56]

Clearly, Llewellyn Park was the precedent for Olmsted and Vaux. Its principal designer was the architect Alexander Jackson Davis, an early influence on Olmsted. Davis was also a close friend of Andrew Jackson Downing.[57] Since Calvert Vaux had been Downing's assistant at the time Llewellyn Park was being developed, Olmsted had a rich resource to draw upon for the plan of Riverside, Illinois (Fig. 21). In 1868 Olmsted was invited by Emery Childs, an eastern businessman, to survey 1600 acres of land near Chicago. Childs had purchased the land for the Riverside Improvement Company. Most of this tract was contained in a single undeveloped parcel on the Des Plaines River. The location was the first stop on the Quincy Railroad outside of Chicago. The investment, a speculative venture, would be augmented, Childs believed, by comprehensive social and physical planning.[58]

What emerged was Olmsted's first and most satisfactory community plan. He was, of course, to do others—such as Tarrytown, New York (Fig. 22); Roland Park, Baltimore; and Pinehurst, North Carolina. The first two were more in the nature of subdivisions than community plans and Pinehurst was not of the same comprehensive scale as Riverside. Riverside remains one of America's foremost examples of nineteenth-century community design and a clear, early roadmark in the development of the garden city throughout the western world.[59]

To achieve a satisfactory environment, Olmsted and Vaux made several recommendations. Among the first was the construction of a parkway "from two hundred to six hundred feet wide, extending from the city [Chicago]." The national economic depression of 1873 prevented the construction of this parkway. But it did not interfere with the completion of much of the original site-plan.[60]

In planning Riverside, Olmsted addressed himself to the problem of rural isolation induced by poor roads. Women living in the countryside, he noted, "are far more confined . . . by the walls of their dwelling, than their town sisters, and mainly because they have been obliged to train and adapt themselves during a large part of the year to an avoidance of the annoyances and fatigue of going out." To remedy this situation, he urged liberal investment of funds in order to drain the entire area of Riverside so that the twin scourges of good roads—"water and frost"—would be avoided.[61]

If a principal inadequacy of the countryside was poor roads, a chief failure of cities—in which roads were generally better constructed—was that urban streets were wholly developed for commercial—not residential—uses. The gridiron system of street planning evident in most nineteenth-century American cities and in their extensions encouraged fast through-traffic and commercial building. Urban technology tended to ignore and destroy the ecological systems and forms of nature, which were irregular, not geometrical. In planning the internal road system of Riverside, Olmsted and Vaux stressed that speed would be "of less importance than comfort and convenience of movement." And they favored "gracefully-curved lines, generous spaces, and the absence of sharp corners, the idea being to suggest and imply leisure, contemplativeness and happy tranquillity."[62]

Finally, Riverside would be distinguished by a physical form that encouraged communal activities. The public land of Riverside was organized in such a way that "families dwelling within a suburb [would] enjoy much in common, and all the more enjoy it because it is in common." For this social, as well as ecological and aesthetic, purpose, the Des Plaines River became the organizing land form around which to structure a system of open space. Most of Riverside's generous allotment of open space —700 acres—consisted of the commons, playgrounds, and public walks and drives protecting the ecological and visual integrity of that river. The strength of the open-space plan, still apparent, lay in the variety of uses made possible by its design.[63]

3. Campus Plans

Just as the suburb was a design for a new social alternative, Olmsted's plan for campuses envisaged a new educational environment within which to train an improved national leadership. Andrew Jackson Downing had already perceived the need for a new type of higher education in the 1850's. Downing's plan for an agricultural college in New York State was an effort to remedy the ignorance and isolation of rural life. Nothing was more shocking to American intellectuals in the 1850's and '60's than to discover that a commitment to Jeffersonian agrarianism had failed to produce viable communities and sophisticated leadership.[64]

It was Downing's authority in all matters pertaining to agriculture that led the New York State legislature to sponsor his study of the relationship of higher education to farming. His report advocated the creation of an agricultural college. He pointed to the primitive, frontierlike behavior of most farmers, who lacked any scientific understanding of their pursuits. It was typical of farmers, Downing wrote, to thrust "wires up the nostrils of sheep, to remove insects in the head" or to drive "a knife in the stomach of an ox, to relieve him from gas."[65]

Downing was not arguing, however, simply for the establishment of a college devoted to the teaching of agricultural techniques. The overriding need was for a new institution devoted to a total understanding of natural processes—what today would be referred to as "environmental study." The curriculum would include such subjects as natural philosophy, natural history, geology, mineralogy, chemistry, mathematics, engineering, practical surveying, botany, horticulture, veterinary art, anatomy, history, law, and general science. Such a curriculum would produce a professional planner, for instance, well trained in matters pertaining to the physical and social environment.[66]

Downing's proposal was taken up nationally in the United States Congress by Justin Morrill, a member of the House of Representatives from Vermont. Morrill understood the full intent of Downing's proposal and came to appreciate Olmsted's ability as a physical and social designer. Olmsted was to rely greatly on Morrill for support of his design for the Capitol in Washington, D.C. Morrill, who served for forty-four consecutive years in Congress (1854–98)—twelve as a Representative and thirty-two as a Senator—was in complete sympathy with Olmsted's goals. Both men shared Downing's belief in the need for a new system of education based on scientific thought.[67]

Morrill first introduced legislation for a national agricultural college on December 14, 1857, but it was not until July 2, 1862, that President Lincoln signed the bill, which had been reintroduced in each successive session of the Congress. The Morrill Act attempted to codify the concept, shared by Downing and Olmsted, that "scientific knowledge ought in some way to be made more useful to the daily occupations of life than had previously been thought possible, and that the educational system of the country ought to contribute more directly to that end than it was then doing."[68]

Significantly, Morrill did not intend that the land-grant college

36

become preoccupied exclusively with agricultural matters. Rather, it was meant to be an alternative to the more traditional American university dominant in the middle of the nineteenth century. "It is perhaps needless to say," Morrill noted,

> that these Colleges were not established or endowed for the sole purpose of teaching agriculture. Their object was to give an opportunity for those engaged in industrial pursuits to obtain some knowledge of the practical sciences related to agriculture and the mechanic arts; such as they could not then obtain at most of our institutions called classical Colleges, where the languages, Greek and Latin, French and German, absorbed perhaps two-thirds of all the time of the students while in college.[69]

Morrill and Olmsted understood one another. They shared similar views on such related matters as religion, the responsibility of the state in matters of the public environment, and the role of the planner in the environmental process. Thus it was easy for Olmsted to translate the Morrill Act into a plan for the University of Maine in 1867, as he had for the new agricultural college at Amherst a year before. His report made it clear that he viewed the campus as more than a place where knowledge was imparted—much more than a cluster of buildings. It was, for a significant period of each student's life, a total environment, having an incalculable effect on future attitudes. "It is absolutely essential to the success of the institution," Olmsted wrote, "that during the four years in which students shall be subject to its direct influence, certain tastes, inclinations and habits shall be established with them. . . . So far as the College shall fail in this respect it must fail to accomplish the sole end had in view in its endowment."[70]

All of Olmsted's campus plans completed between 1865 and 1868—for Berkeley (Fig. 4), Maine, Amherst, and Gallaudet College (Fig. 23)—reflected the "total community" ideal of the New England village setting. The antithesis of this concept is seen in the formal, regular pattern of English universities such as Cambridge and Oxford. Instead of the large stone buildings and monasticlike qualities of the English university, Olmsted favored small, detached buildings made of wood, "models of healthy, cheerful, convenient family homes." In designing classroom facilities, he recommended movable partitions to permit maximum utilization of interior space and future additions to buildings. Plans for recreation included a library, gardens, and an athletic field.[71]

This environment, Olmsted believed, would nurture enlightened leaders. Passage of the Morrill Act—during the Civil War—was facilitated by public reaction to the failure of northern military leadership in such debacles as Bull Run. "It is clearly the intention of the act of congress," he wrote,

> to secure as an incidental advantage of Industrial Colleges, the preparation of a certain number of young men in each state for acting as officers and instructors of volunteer forces, and thus to save the nation from ever again being so completely unprepared for the duty of self-defence as it was found to be at the outbreak of the rebellion.[72]

Such an élite group, Olmsted hoped, would address itself to national matters. The Civil War made this commitment all the more necessary since it was viewed by many Europeans as a failure of democracy. Democratic reconstruction of the nation would demonstrate that America was capable of planning and carrying out policies to meet the needs of an urbanizing and industrializing nation. Functional designs, if aesthetically distinctive, would symbolize the creative capacity of a social democracy.

4. "National" Parks: Yosemite

Olmsted's efforts to preserve the Yosemite Valley in the California Sierras, which he first visited in August 1864, is an example of the kind of national movement that he wished to see championed and directed by a new leadership. Although transportation facilities were primitive at that time and California was still sparsely settled, the Valley and its neighboring Big Tree Grove were attracting hundreds of visitors yearly (Fig. 30). Olmsted saw in the neighboring Valley a great natural resource. It would further the public interest in a variety of ways: as a large outdoor space that future generations would need for recreation, as a source for study by scientists and artists, and as a symbol of national greatness.[73]

The site afforded the viewer a spiritual experience—nature sanctified in a democratic setting. "Mr. Olmsted," wrote the family governess,

> took me to the Sequoias this afternoon. The road lies up a steep ascent covered with beautiful pines and firs and after a ride of five miles through this woodland we suddenly came upon the majestic trunk of a Sequoia. The great beauty of these forest kings is as striking as their size. The bark is a rich golden brown, and immensely thick. . . . It is formed into regular carvings like the Gothic ornaments of a cathedral yet no artificial architecture ever impressed me as much as the grand and simple outlines of these wonderful creations.[74]

By an act approved June 30, 1864, the United States Government granted to the State of California the Yosemite Valley and the Mariposa Big Tree Grove, stipulating that "the State shall accept this grant upon the expressed condition that the premises shall be held for public use, resort, and recreation, and shall be inalienable for all time." The valley and grove were to be administered by the governor through a group of commissioners appointed by him to serve without salary. Olmsted acted as first President of the Commission.[75]

The Commission had two immediate tasks. First, the area had to be surveyed and mapped. This was accomplished by Clarence King and James T. Gardiner, members of the California State Geological Survey. Second, a report on management policy of the grant, with specific recommendations for carrying out the terms, had to be prepared. This Olmsted did.

On August 8, 1865, before a meeting of the Commission, Olmsted read his report. He set forth general principles to guide governmental policy in the preservation of natural resources. In addition, he made very specific recommendations for long-term maintenance of Yosemite Valley. He thus articulated for his generation a philosophy and a set of working principles for the creation of state and national parks. The report was not published by the California legislature. But its spirit—values shared by many of Olmsted's contemporaries—survived, later to be reflected in the establishment of the United States Park Service.

IV

THE

POLITICS OF

DESIGN

The many large disappointments that Olmsted suffered—the number of public projects that he advocated and which were not adopted—would seem to indicate that many battles were lost owing to political ineptitude on his part. Such an interpretation would conform to the myth that he was politically naive—a babe in the woods controlled by hungry and vicious politicians—and would be misleading. A more accurate appraisal of Olmsted's career suggests, to the contrary, that his successes were in fact only made possible because of the considerable political support he could often muster. He consistently sought to use whatever political mechanisms were available to turn proposals into realities. He remained keenly, and painfully, aware that in a democracy all matters of environmental planning and design, because they were based upon hard issues rooted in social and economic conditions, inevitably became political matters. Olmsted's record of achievement in Boston after his defeat in New

York City was owing to the social and political support he found there.[76] Boston, unlike New York, still retained an effective intellectual and social élite committed to large-scale environmental planning. In Boston (Fig. 36), from 1878–95 Olmsted was able to effect a remarkable park system for the city (Fig. 32) and to initiate, with his young partner, Charles Eliot, a greater metropolitan open-space plan (Fig. 37).

1.   A Successful Campaign: Niagara Falls

From his new base in Boston, Olmsted also demonstrated political skill in helping to establish an international reservation at Niagara Falls. The need to preserve the Falls was not new. As early as 1835 two visitors from Scotland had urged that Niagara Falls "be deemed the property of civilized mankind." Increasingly, visitors described the Falls as the epitome of natural beauty and industrial power—the symbols of a democratic nation. However, it was these very same qualities that attracted commercial interests and threatened the survival of the Falls as public property.[77]

In 1869, the noted landscape painter Frederick Church had brought "the rapidly approaching ruins of its characteristic scenery" to Olmsted's attention. Whereas in the 1830's the Falls were popular simply for their magnificence, by the 1860's they had become commercialized and were threatened with the intrusion of industry. Olmsted was concerned that the natural setting of the American side—Goat Island in particular—be preserved for future generations. The physical environment of the Falls—the uniqueness of its microclimate—had led to a special type of natural growth and visual effect on the island. "All these distinctive qualities," Olmsted wrote,

> the great variety of the indigenous perennials and annuals,
> the rare beauty of the old woods, and the exceeding loveliness
> of the rock foliage,—I believe to be a direct effect of the Falls,
> and as much a part of its majesty as the mist-cloud and the
> rainbow.[78]

It was not, however, until 1879 that an appeal to preserve the Falls was made to the Governor-General of Canada, Lord Dufferin. Responding to the urgent request of Church, Olmsted, and the architect Henry H. Richardson, Lord Dufferin began to work on the problem politically. Almost simultaneously, the New York State legislature authorized a complete survey of the American side of the site under the direction of Olmsted and James T. Gardiner, at that time Director of the New York State Geological Survey. Since Gardiner had assisted in the topographical analysis of Yosemite Valley, his cooperation represented a rare instance of continued team effort in public land preservation and use.

After a comprehensive review of the subject, Olmsted and Gardiner submitted an elaborate and detailed report urging the acquisition by New York State of as much land as was necessary for the protection of the characteristic environment of the Falls, to be held in trust forever for the people. Unnecessary landscape gardening and formal ornamentation were to be avoided and natural conditions of the site, as far as possible, restored and maintained.[79]

The importance of this report and the eventual acquisition of the land on both sides of the Falls to which it led cannot be overestimated. It was, and remains, an almost unprecedented act of international cooperation. Two nations had agreed to the creation of an armament-free border. As the Commissioners of the State Survey put it:

Niagara is not simply the crowning glory of New York State, but is the highest distinction of the Nation, and of the continent of America. No other like gift of Nature equally holds the interest of the world or operates as an inducement for men to cross the sea.[80]

By 1879, however, Olmsted knew that writing a report was one thing and that having it realized at all intact was quite another. Only a year before this he had been forced out of his position as Landscape Architect for the New York City Department of Parks. Now he wished to have a major project—Niagara Falls—sanctioned by the New York State legislature, fully as political an arena as the municipal government that had rejected him. "It is a big [planning] problem," he wrote to Gardiner. ". . . All practicable room to work in should be secured."[81]

To achieve such a professional goal, however, a major political obstacle had to be overcome—that of private interests powerfully entrenched in the legislature. A campaign had to be mounted in order to counterbalance the pressure of industrialists and manufacturers who saw the Falls as an exploitable resource. The steps taken by Olmsted, Gardiner, and their close supporter, the Harvard scholar Charles Eliot Norton, were eminently realistic and political. If their tactics differed from those of more institutionalized political groups, the difference was owing to the fact that their principal client was the public—not any private—interest. An example of the public-interest approach was their solicitation of the signatures of some of the most distinguished citizens in the Anglo-American world, on a petition signed by 700 of them. "Probably no document of a similar character," wrote one chronicler, "ever bore such a distinguished list of names."[82]

Nor were personal contacts neglected. Olmsted reported one that was successful:

> Mr. Woodruff is an elderly gentleman. . . . He had some years ago a fierce newspaper war with the hackmen of Niagara and is a heated partisan of general public interests in the Falls as against the local robbers. He wrote to Gov[erno]r Robinson urging him to favor the International Park suggestion. Robinson thanked him and adopted a part of the language of his letter in the message. He was glad to see me and very soon came to the point of saying, "I will give my time, influence and money if need be to favor the scheme."[83]

Another means of public persuasion was the use of commissioned publications. Olmsted had little time in the post-Civil War period to continue with his social investigations and writings. Since he could not undertake such studies, he encouraged the work of a young Unitarian minister turned journalist, Jonathan Baxter Harrison, whose views on social matters he shared; with Olmsted's guidance, Harrison in 1882 had completed perhaps

44

the most extensive survey of southern society since Olmsted's in the 1850's. "What is the state of the Niagara business?" Charles Norton asked. "It is almost time to get Harrison at work."[84]

And work he did. Harrison, in a series of articles published in the *Boston Advertiser* and other newspapers and reprinted in pamphlet form for national circulation, caught the essence of the struggle. To the interest group most opposed to the preservation of the Falls, he wrote:

> You see, gentlemen capitalists and manufacturers, the laborer must toil, *happily,* or you may all come to grief together, and capital must supply and maintain the conditions of beauty and happiness for him. Labor, directed and ennobled by the ideal, moral or spiritual element, creates everything; but a democratic civilization, based on the labor of a class of serfs of the mine and mill, whose toil is unwilling, degraded, and faithless, would not be likely to endure long in a world where the deepest meaning of everything is moral.[85]

Although Harrison's writings and other political measures helped to keep the proposal alive, they could not by themselves compel a reluctant legislature either to acquire the land by eminent domain or to appropriate the funds for that acquisition. Executive action was needed to mobilize support, but the new governor, Alonzo B. Cornell, in 1882 considered the project a luxury, neither essential to the health and welfare of the larger community nor in the interests of improved international relations.[86]

The situation changed dramatically with the election of Grover Cleveland as governor in January 1883. One of Cleveland's chief advisers was a long-time friend and supporter of Olmsted, William Dorsheimer. With Dorsheimer's assistance, success was assured. "I have a telegram of congratulations . . . on the passing of the Niagara Bill by the Assembly by a large majority," Olmsted wrote happily to Norton on March 14.[87] On April 30, the bill passed the Senate and on the same day was signed by Governor Cleveland. Two days later, the governor appointed a five-man commission to supervise the arrangements. The president of the commission was Dorsheimer.

The major political obstacles had thus been overcome by orthodox political methods. But then began the onerous task of appraisal and condemnation of existing private facilities in the area. It was not until two years later that final settlement with owners had been made and rights acquired to the land surrounding the Falls, as well as to Goat Island. The grounds around the Falls were officially opened to the public on July 15, 1885. Soon after this event, Dorsheimer turned to Olmsted to undertake a study and long-range plan of the Niagara Reservation, with special emphasis on Goat Island (Fig. 31). Calvert Vaux was a co-author of the resultant report. Discussing the assignment with Dorsheimer, Olmsted summarized the focus of his concern: "[to provide] as amply as practicable for great throngs of people . . . to preserve and develop a particular character of natural scenery on a great scale avoiding as much as possible all manifestation of art, human labor, or human purpose."[88]

It is clear that in the drive to restore and preserve Niagara Falls for the public, Olmsted's role was eminently political. Why, then, had he been so badly defeated in battles with the political infrastructure of New York City—the nation's most important metropolis. Was it because he was a "romantic enthusiast," "a quack," a "wholly impractical man"—terms frequently applied to him by his contemporaries.[89] Not at all. Rather, it was because he was "political" in a larger sense than party politics; he was concerned with the social welfare of the city. Olmsted was caricatured by these epithets—and even threatened physically—because he was an obstacle and a threat to some of the political leadership of the city. The undermining of his influence was to some a necessity, since his objectives conflicted with the social and economic thrust of New York City politics in the last third of the nineteenth century.

How then had Olmsted been able to survive for more than two decades as the major planner and designer for New York City? The answer is that during that period he had had a viable political base. His initial appointment as Superintendent and Architect-in-Chief of Central Park stemmed from his national reputation as a social critic; his views were shared by leading members of New York City's social and political life. When invited to apply for the post of Superintendent, he was advised to obtain the support of influential friends. "Accordingly, the next day," he recalled, "I was looking for my friends in New York. At that season they were much scattered, but I found one who took up the matter warmly, and my application was in a few days fortified by a number of weighty signatures." The list had included leading social, economic, and literary figures of that day.[90]

2. A Major Defeat: Parks and Politics

There are many specific factors that contributed to Olmsted's defeat in New York City. But the fundamental one was the disintegration of the social-political alliance that had generally supported his efforts there in the period 1857–78, leading to an abandonment of the earlier commitment to comprehensive planning. After this time, he was compelled to seek out other localities and new patrons to sustain his work. Furthermore, it is clear that wherever Olmsted practiced after 1878, including Boston, certain basic changes took place in his planning, for the disintegration of his base of power in New York City was symptomatic of a massive social shift nationally in terms of industrialization.

The larger social basis of popular understanding and belief in the need for environmental planning was losing ground rapidly before the onslaught of a new national ideology, social Darwinism, dedicated to the principal of survival of the fittest. When Charles Darwin's classic study of the principles of evolution, *Origin of Species,* was published in 1859, it received an immediate favorable reaction among Olmsted's social coterie. Olmsted, who later became a friend of the English scientist, always considered him to be a preeminent genius of the age. In part, the book was so well received because it incorporated the research of the American botanist Asa Gray, a relative of Charles Loring Brace and an associate of Olmsted. Also, the work offered clear evidence for the separation of scientific from religious thought that had taken place in New England. Most important, however, was the support it gave to those who believed in the ability of mankind to progress through a better understanding of the interrelationship of living things with their environment.[91]

But this interpretation of Darwinian thought was, as a major intellectual opinion, short-lived. It was eclipsed in the 1870's by the theory expounded in the writings of Darwin's countryman Herbert Spencer that struggle for survival was the normal state of social behavior, in which it was inevitable that the weak would die and the strong prevail. This system of thought—Social Darwinism—pervasive in every aspect of American society, bolstered a laissez-faire economy, supported a racist belief that sanctioned the abandonment of the newly freed black people, by the 1890's strengthened an imperialist ideology, and was antithetical to comprehensive planning and design.[92]

The nation had failed to fashion a social and intellectual leadership capable of extending to the national environment the principles of planning and design that Olmsted had applied in Central Park and elsewhere. If that portion of the population privileged by birth or good fortune to acquire wealth and knowledge would not or could not support him, his larger goals were simply unattainable within the established political structure. "And what stands in the way of this benefaction," Olmsted asked rhetorically:

> . . . The coarseness and rudeness and brutality of the population that never leaves the town? Not so good sirs. But the indifference of such men—lovers of art, patrons of art, lovers of nature, patrons of nature on a wall.[93]

The Civil War had only widened the gap between national needs, as Olmsted perceived them, and the possibility of their fulfillment. His experiences with the Sanitary Commission during the war had dramatized how serious deficiencies in national planning led to wastefulness and loss of lives. This awareness in turn converted him to the proposition that power needed to be shifted from the states to the national government. Before the war, *Putnam's Monthly Magazine* had championed states rights even to the extent of defending the arguments of the South's chief political theorist, John C. Calhoun. "With the end at which Mr. Calhoun aims," the periodical noted, "—the arrest of centralization—we cordially sympathize." However, the experience of the Civil War compelled a complete revision of this position. As Olmsted explained it: "We could not suffer 'States Rights' to accomplish secession." He soon discovered among friends who had been advocates of local self-government a new bond: "that we were one and all thorough converts to Federalism."[94]

Nor was this conversion simply the result of the Civil War. Olmsted's extensive experience with local government and urban politics in New York City from 1857 until the outbreak of the war had convinced him of the need for greater centralization of planning authority in a growing metropolis. The Board of Commissioners of Central Park, to which Olmsted was responsible during this period, offered the best hope for a city planning agency. Its authority prior to and immediately after the war was considerable, with power over such matters as parks, streets, and the general development of unsettled portions of the city (Fig. 88). Without the delegation of such powers to the Board by the state, Central Park would never have come into existence.

However, it was clear, years before Olmsted was forced out by the commissioners of Central Park, that the granting of such authority to a board of laymen, appointed by the mayor for a fixed term of office, was unsatisfactory and impeded the larger goals of environmental planning. Venality was not the cause; Olmsted himself often noted that—certainly when compared to other city agencies—the conduct of the commissioners of Central Park was unusually honest. "Even under the [Tammany Hall] Ring," he wrote,

> no commissioner was the richer for the position he held and the Comptroller [of New York City] who had a special motive and the best opportunity and all desirable means of exposing dishonesty has never made any definite charge against them of worse crimes than bad taste and extravagance.[95]

The problem was not one of dishonesty, but rather that the commission had become politicized and subversive of the best interests of the public environment. This subversion took place on at least three different levels, each related to the larger issue of the role of the professional within the political process. First, there was the matter of political patronage. The Board had the power to hire and fire personnel on all levels, and decisions more often than not were made on the basis of political expediency. This placed Olmsted in the position of having to manage a large army of men without sufficient authority to regulate their performance.

A second drawback, which related to the first, and which emerged more clearly after the Civil War, was the refusal of the Board to allocate sufficient funds for the development of professional park management. As the planning principles that had guided the park's original design became more distant and were submerged in the ideology of social Darwinism, a crisis was reached. Without adequate professional assistance and controls, the park could not be maintained.

The final—and ultimately fatal—detrimental aspect had to do with future planning of New York City's undeveloped land, including that acquired by the city's annexation of part of Westchester County in 1873. Olmsted crossed swords with the Board when he publicly argued against development of the area until large-scale planning and design had taken place with respect to transportation, sewerage, roads, and open space (Figs. 33, 78).[96]

He lost this battle and as a consequence was forced out of the New York City Department of Parks. A basic change in his professional career resulted, as we have noted. For instance, after 1878 Olmsted worked primarily as a private planner and designer. He had, of course, done private work previously, and he did not cease working for public agencies thereafter; but before 1878 his principal employer was the public sector and his particular role in New York City compelled him to participate actively in its daily life. After 1878, when Olmsted worked extensively for public agencies, as in Boston, it was always as a private consultant—only rarely as a public servant. When a public employee—that is, engaged on a salaried rather than fee basis—he served for limited periods as a consultant, as at Morningside Park, New York City, without any direct responsibil-

50

ity for step-by-step supervision of construction. When Charles Norton asked Olmsted to find public employment for a deserving friend, Olmsted replied: "My position is now only advisory as to any of the works with which I have to do. I have made no appointments and but one nomination in several years."[97] Not even in Boston were his planning concepts to take firm root.

But Olmsted was not any less the social architect. His extraordinarily successful private practice left little time from the 1880's on for direct participation in social and political reform movements or for any major publication about American society. However, we do have the published works of Olmsted's close associate, Jonathan B. Harrison, from the period when the two men were in close collaboration on a variety of matters. Olmsted supported Harrison because, as we know, he himself was so overburdened. He could encourage the work of Harrison and others, with the knowledge that through their efforts his social principles would reach a national audience.

Harrison's most comprehensive statement—the one that most closely paralleled Olmsted's own views—was his *Notes on Industrial Conditions* (1887). The fear of social revolution caused Olmsted and his friend Norton to sponsor the study. "I believe," Olmsted wrote Norton, that "the employers in the large corporations here, are not in the least disposed to fair discussion. They are generally taking the sea captain's view and regard every grievance and aspiration of the working man as unreasonable and unnatural. The great body of working men are necessarily in a corresponding attitude."[98]

Harrison's conclusions, following his survey, were even more critical of the failure of the new industrial class to consider the needs of the laboring class of the nation. The hard-working poor, he wrote, "can make no provision for sickness or old age. Even honesty and self-respect are denied them, for misfortune sooner or later compels them . . . to accept the charity which is often scattered with lavish hand by those who have been deaf to all the requirements of justice. To these men and women life is empty of hope and beauty and tenderness. They live and die without faith in God or man."[99]

Although shorn of the optimism of the 1850's—by the experience of the Civil War and the omnipresence of a new industrial society—the publication clings to the idealism of that earlier period. The most poignant theme of the book is the painful recognition of the impact of the war on the social development of the nation. Reconstruction had failed to carry out the Civil War ideals of freedom and equality that had motivated that conflict. In retrospect, it seemed as though the conflict itself unexpectedly had led to undesirable social changes.

V

OLD

PRINCIPLES—

NEW DESIGNS

For Harrison, Olmsted, and many others, America had failed to pursue national principles that were unifying and uplifting. The nation had neither sustained the spirit nor provided the political mechanisms to fulfill those aims of social democracy for which a most costly war had been fought. For Olmsted, who understood how critical New York City's leadership was to the rest of the nation,[100] his defeat there was most traumatic. However, he refused to surrender either his principles or his hope. And, fortunately, he had the capacity to reassert his position by turning once again to first principles.

1. Ecology Reaffirmed

Where to begin? The essence of Olmsted's theory of environmental planning was a reverence for the fundamental characteristics of all living matter. This was basic to the concepts of scientific farming, which Olmsted had practiced. If ecological laws were violated, there was little hope for social planning based on a belief in a rational relationship between human beings and the physical environment. In this context, nothing was more disturbing to Olmsted in the 1880's than the increased use of exotic plant materials for decorative purposes. It was the Gilded Age's horticultural equivalent of social Darwinism. Plant materials were used as symbols of the belief in the survival of the fittest, displayed for their rarity and high cost rather than for their intrinsic characteristics—that is, their ecological relationship to the site.[101]

To offset this trend, Olmsted supported the botanical efforts of Lester F. Ward, who was to become the principal critic of social Darwinism in the last third of the nineteenth century. Ward provided an intellectual basis for a new generation of social and physical reformers. Born in 1842 in the Middle West on the Des Plaines River, Ward was the most comprehensive social theorist in the second half of the nineteenth century, linking nature to the reform spirit of the antebellum era. The origin of his social concepts, like Olmsted's, was in natural science.[102]

In a report published in 1881, two years before the appearance of *Dynamic Sociology,* Ward's first major sociological work, Olmsted commended Ward for his contribution to botany. Olmsted was urging the administrators of the nation's capital to undertake, as a national example of urban planning, a comprehensive system of tree planting in harmony with the city's climate. "If well followed up in the care of the trees," Olmsted predicted,

> the results will give Washington a distinction among the capital towns of the world—a distinction original, representative, and historic. . . .
> . . . [And he advised that] those [readers] who wish to have a more extended list of what may be looked for, as well as all interested, whether as botanists or as lovers of nature in local, annual, perennial plants, will find the best of aid in a Government publication prepared by Mr. Lester F. Ward, of the Smithsonian Institution.[103]

54

It was for a similar reason that in 1889 Olmsted and Harrison, who was at that time Corresponding Secretary of the American Forestry Congress, attacked the popular belief that the thinning of trees was somehow a violation of ecological principles. They recommended that the public, instead of condemning tree-cutting in urban parks and seeking legislation to prevent such acts, take the position that wherever no thinning occurred "there is ground for presumption—a very strong presumption—that the management is ignorant or neglectful of its most important duty." Public education in sound ecological principles and "natural" gardening also had motivated Olmsted to join with the noted horticulturist and botanist Charles Sprague Sargent in the planning and design of the Arnold Arboretum (Fig. 41) and in the publication in 1887 of the periodical *Garden and Forest.* In addition, we have noted that he planned Lynn Woods, Lynn, Massachusetts (Fig. 20), and Iroquois Park, Louisville, Kentucky (Fig. 64), in part to exemplify this scientific principle of forestry in urban areas.[104]

2. Scientific Forestry: Biltmore

The fundamental principle of conservation of natural resources motivated Olmsted to work with men of wealth. He hoped to persuade American millionaires to establish planned environments to serve as models in much the same way that the aristocratic English estates of the eighteenth and nineteenth centuries had become prototypes of landscape planning. His greatest challenge was George W. Vanderbilt's request in 1888 for advice and guidance in the planning and design of an estate—Biltmore—near Asheville, North Carolina. The relationship between Olmsted and the Vanderbilt family was well established. They had been neighbors on Staten Island during the 1850's, and in 1886 Olmsted had collaborated on a design for the family mausoleum on Staten Island and for a subdivision near Lenox, Massachusetts.[105]

But Biltmore was different; it tested all of Olmsted's knowledge, ingenuity, and strength. Although Vanderbilt's original intention was to have a healthy winter and spring residence for himself and his mother, it soon became something much more ambitious

(Figs. 27, 28). He asked Olmsted's guidance as to how he could "turn the larger part of the property to good account, as a matter of business, in a manner that would allow him to take some pleasure in its management and that would make the scenery and the advantages for a pleasant out-of-doors life not less agreeable than at present." Olmsted recommended a massive project in "forest plantations . . . kept and managed as a commercial forest . . . [and] . . . an Arboretum" as a means of public education in science and art. Vanderbilt took Olmsted's advice, enlarging the estate to approximately 120,000 acres; the project rapidly achieved national attention. "The public is more and more making a resort of the place," Olmsted noted, "and I have never more felt that it is the most permanently important work and the most critical with reference to the future of our profession of all that we have. The most critical and the most difficult."[106]

It was difficult for several reasons. First, there were the objective demands of the plan itself. The social influence of Biltmore was paramount. There was to be a model village for the estate's employees, including a drainage, water, and street system in an area of the country devoid of such amenities; the plan projected, too, a model system of roads for the estate "that can be referred to . . . for all the country" as an example of regional planning; and, finally, Olmsted hoped for a balanced use of the estate both as an archetype of scientific forestry conducted for commercial profit and as an arboretum for ecological and landscape design education.[107]

The second area of difficulty was the opposition Olmsted encountered from Hunt on almost every aspect of the project and the considerable influence Hunt had with Vanderbilt. "Hunt," Olmsted wrote, "is accustomed to have his own way and is more than earnest—is tempestuous—in debate." Olmsted was willing to cooperate on the siting and design of the château (Fig. 29), but not at the expense of other aspects of the project. "The house and all immediately about it will be magnificent," he wrote, "and I dread the contrasting poverty and dwindled character that I fear will be found to generally prevail." Notably, he insisted that Hunt alter his architecture for Biltmore village from a French design to that of the total "New England Ideal" and the street system Olmsted had laid out.[108]

Finally, the project was complicated by the fact that Olmsted was failing in health and unable to meet the large professional obligations that he had assumed. He had to withdraw his personal supervision of Biltmore, which soon fell far short of the goals set for it. Biltmore did, however, affect the history of American forestry in three important ways: first, it gave impetus to Gifford Pinchot's career—Pinchot, who left the project in 1895, went on to become chief of the Division of Forestry of the Department of Agriculture and a pioneer in that field. Second, under Carl Alwin Schenck, whom Pinchot had recommended for the position of chief forester at Biltmore, the Biltmore School of Forestry was founded in 1897, lasting until 1912; it was the first effort of its kind in the country to train scientific foresters. Finally, when Vanderbilt died in 1917, his widow, with an act of wisdom and generosity that Olmsted surely would have applauded, turned over 100,000 acres of the estate to the National Forest Reservation Commission, specifying that it become a national preserve— thereby perpetuating the advancement of the public good that had motivated both her husband and his planner.[109]

3. A New Utopia

Given Olmsted's disastrous experience with the political leadership of New York City—and with that of other cities as well— and the rapid emergence of a new social class in the 1880's and '90's, we understand why he later worked on private estates for men of wealth and power. But planning would have to take place within some new theoretical frame of reference; it could not be based on social Darwinism, the exploitation of man and nature. This tie between social concerns and physical planning was dramatized by Edward Bellamy in his extraordinarily influential novel, *Looking Backward,* published in 1888.

The essence of Bellamy's work, although the author denied it, was indeed retrospective—a nostalgic attempt to recapture the imagined simplicity of an earlier, less complex, more socially responsive New England community. "I am glad," wrote the noted literary figure William Dean Howells, "that he [Bellamy] lived to die at home in Chicopee—in the village environment by which he interpreted the heart of the American nation, and knew how to move it more than any other American author who has lived."[110]

The success and influence of the novel was in large measure owing to the extent to which it responded to widespread concern about the future stability of the nation. The novel was published less than two years after the great labor struggles of 1886, when affairs like the Haymarket episode and the eight-hour strikes in Chicago were still fresh in the public mind. While thousands were reading the novel, with its description of future peace and prosperity, there occurred the bloody strikes in the Carnegie Steel Works at Homestead, Pennsylvania, and in the Pullman plant at Chicago. The book seemed to provide an ideal solution to the social ills brought about by class polarization.

Bellamy's utopia was planned, humane, efficient, and cooperative, in contrast with what seemed to be a haphazard, ruthless, wasteful, and competitive way of life. It was a reiteration of the utopian ideals that had moved American reformers in 1850. But the structure of Bellamy's society was antithetical to that of the antebellum period. Indeed, Bellamy urged that utopia could only become a reality through the methods of big business. "Early in the last century," spoke one of the heroes of the novel from the perspective of the year 2000,

> the evolution was completed by the final consolidation of the entire capital of the nation. The industry and commerce of the country, ceasing to be conducted by a set of irresponsible corporations and syndicates of private persons at their caprice and for their profit, were intrusted to a single syndicate representing the people to be conducted in the common interest for the common profit.[111]

It is more than likely that Olmsted and Bellamy were acquaintances. They were both active in the same social circles in Boston in the 1880's and were perhaps drawn together by Sylvester Baxter, an admirer of them both. Particularly striking was Bellamy's selection of Asheville, North Carolina, as the locale for an early version of the book, rather than Boston, as in the final edition. But it is unnecessary to seek out such connections. The impact of *Looking Backward* is sufficient. It was one of those rare books that spurred men to action and was particularly attractive to members of Olmsted's social circle. One hundred and fifty Nationalist clubs had been established all over the country by October 1890, advocating a practical application of Bellamy's ideas. In the Boston area, such close friends of Olmsted as Charles Eliot Norton and Edward Everett Hale became strong supporters of Bellamy, discovering in *Looking Backward* a projection of their own social ideals.[112]

And with good reason. Olmsted's generation of reformers believed deeply in the symbiosis between society and environment. *Looking Backward* relies heavily on vivid descriptions of urban scenes to document the failures of the past. Boston, like most American cities, Bellamy declared, was diseased:

> From the black doorways and windows of the rookeries, on every side came gusts of fetid air. The streets and alleys reeked with the effluvia of a slave ship's between-decks. As I passed I had glimpses within of pale babies gasping out their lives amid sultry stenches, of hopeless-faced women deformed by hardship, retaining of womanhood no trait save weakness, while from the windows leered girls with brows of brass.[113]

Utopia was also translated into physical terms. By the year 2000, Bellamy projected, Boston could be transformed. He wrote:

> At my feet lay a great city. Miles of broad streets, shaded by trees and lined with fine buildings, for the most part in continuous blocks but set in larger or smaller inclosures, stretched in every direction. Every quarter contained large open squares filled with trees, among which statues glistened and fountains flashed in the late afternoon sun. Public buildings of a colossal size and an architectural grandeur

unparalleled in my day raised their stately piles on every side. Surely I had never seen this city nor one comparable to it before.[114]

In Bellamy's utopia there would be no poverty, no crime, no violence, no insanity, and the city of the year 2000 would be a place where recreation was almost as important as work and public education had the highest priority. In sum, it was a physical complex embodying the antebellum principle that the public good was central to the well-being of society and that private greed must be eradicated. "We might," Bellamy wrote,

> indeed, have much larger incomes, individually, if we chose so to use the surplus of our product, but we prefer to expend it upon public works and pleasures in which all share, upon public halls and buildings, art galleries, bridges, statuary, means of transit, and the convenience of our cities, great musical and theatrical exhibitions, and in providing on a vast scale for the recreations of the people. . . . At home we have comfort but the splendor of our life is, on its social side, that which we share with our fellows.[115]

While the utopian message of the late 1880's was identical to that of the 1850's, the governmental structure and physical form of the city to be were not. The romantic, decentralized idealism of the 1850's had been transformed into a highly structured, centralized form reflected in monumental buildings contained within a regular pattern of public squares and uniform blocks. Bellamy's principal argument was that the organization of industry, which had revolutionized American life, would become the basis for restructuring the American city. Most appealing to Olmsted and others was the hope it offered of freeing the professional planner and designer from political interference, as, indeed, industry and business had been freed during the second half of the nineteenth century.

A most direct link between the application of Bellamy's theory and Olmsted's work was Sylvester Baxter, a devoted disciple of Bellamy, who saw in park, city, and regional planning the most immediate application of Nationalist theories. Born in 1850, educated in Leipzig, Baxter became in the 1880's a chief organizer of Nationalist clubs in the Boston area and elsewhere. He sought to transfer this social idealism to the comprehensive planning of open spaces. Olmsted, quick to appreciate Baxter's efforts, wrote: "I am following your work for the parks closely and think it most judicious."[116]

Baxter became a prime figure in defending all of Olmsted's work in Boston and in establishing with Olmsted's protégé, Charles Eliot, criteria for regional open-space planning, which in extent and area transcended the traditional city. It was an effort to think organizationally and systematically on a scale that most resembled the large industrial combinations of the nineteenth century. Baxter was pleased to report in *Garden and Forest* in 1891 that "a definite movement for a metropolitan park system has at last been set on foot" in the greater Boston area. A year later, with Baxter as secretary, the Boston Metropolitan Park Commission was organized as an effort at regional government and comprehensive planning. The commission came to control 10,000 acres of parks and public reservations, 30 miles of river banks, 8 miles of seashore, and 27 miles of boulevards and parkways. In the 1890's Baxter was a regular contributor to *Garden and Forest*. He was as staunch a supporter of Olmsted's theories as he was of Bellamy's. For him, the theories were interchangeable.[117]

4. A New Campus Form

It was inevitable that this change in physical form would soon reflect itself in Olmsted's designs for university campuses. The last third of the nineteenth century was particularly notable for the founding of universities by men of wealth. And it was logical that the designs reflected a more formal and structured view of the world. In 1886, the multimillionaire Leland Stanford invited the Olmsted firm to provide a master plan for the campus named in memory of his only child, Leland Stanford, Jr., who had died two years before of a disease described as "brain fever."

It soon became clear that few of Olmsted's recommendations would be applied. Stanford, an example of nineteenth-century industrial-political success, had none of Vanderbilt's respect for Olmsted's professional or creative ability. The difference was owing, perhaps, to the "newness" of the money: Vanderbilt had inherited his fortune, Stanford had made his in the junglelike warfare of railroad enterprise. Stanford's wish was less for a well-planned and -designed campus than for a monument that would have "a healthy growth for a thousand years." Olmsted characterized the intent: "Governor Stanford's Universitatory. That is not any word half big enough for his ideas of what it is to be."[118]

Still, Olmsted looked forward to the project as a challenge. It was a large site—some 7000 acres at Menlo Park, Palo Alto, California. It offered an opportunity to create a meaningful institution in an undeveloped region characterized by a hot, dry climate with which he had little experience. He hoped to persuade Stanford to turn a large part of the site into an arboretum containing the indigenous shrubs and trees of California. To conform with the climatic conditions of the site, he planned to dispense with eastern plant materials and to introduce functional and attractive man-made ones. Much to his disappointment, Olmsted found that Stanford would dictate the basic selection of the site, urge the adoption of "New England trees and turf," and reject the idea of an arboretum. Eventually, Olmsted felt compelled to resign from the project "to avoid responsibility for what was done," for he was unable to obtain even minimal cooperation as to the implementation of various phases of the design as finally agreed upon.[119]

The campus (Fig. 5) was designed as a quadrangle surrounding a common court, framed by low, long buildings. This was a striking departure from Olmsted's previous campus designs (Fig. 4), even in the light of the variance in climates. Olmsted's most distinctive contribution to the campus was related to its ecological and aesthetic features. Stanford apparently accepted his judgment regarding the organization of buildings and walks around the quadrangle—that is, they were to be arranged in terms of the microclimate of the site. Although the basic form of the campus was that of older English or eastern American universities, Stanford agreed to forego the use of turf in this hot, dry climate. Instead, Olmsted recommended a special form of cement for surface topping, which was both functional and attractive. Stanford finally agreed to the use of natural materials—plants, shrubs, and trees—most suitable to the site.[120]

Although the Stanfords could usually be influenced in regard to decorative detail, Olmsted was unable to make the governor understand his concept of beauty in landscape. Failure to educate clients like the Stanfords troubled Olmsted greatly in the 1880's and '90's. Writing to a leading critic of art and architecture, who had just set forth a definition of landscape beauty, Olmsted complained "that one has only to read it and accept it. Yet hardly any body I have to deal with does accept it. How can you account for the rarity of a taste for organized beauty among people otherwise cultivated?"[121]

Although aesthetics had always played an important role in Olmsted's work, it received greater emphasis after 1878. The social and ecological objectives of his plans were less apparent. In his increasing concern with landscape beauty, Olmsted was defending the most obvious rejection—visual—of his multifaceted understanding of environmental planning. His efforts were also explained by others—more frequently in professional and aesthetic terms than in any other way. "If landscape gardening," wrote Olmsted's colleague, Charles S. Sargent, "in its development is one of the arts, it should certainly rank with other professions. Few will deny that the transformation of a series of rock ledges into the succession of smiling landscapes which unite to form the consistent picture now presented by Central Park, is as truly the work of an artist as would be the painting of one of these landscapes on a bit of canvas."[122]

5. "The White City"

Certainly Sargent, as a leading proponent of the social importance of plant materials, knew that art was only one of the multiple factors that constituted environmental planning. "Why," he asked, "do men die while the tulip trees and the white oaks and the sequoias seem to live perpetually?"[123] But he, like others, was subscribing—perhaps unconsciously—to the most convenient idiom of the age. Nowhere was this more apparent than at the Chicago World's Fair—the Columbian Exposition of 1893 (Fig. 3) —Olmsted's last major public urban design project. This event— an opportunity to commemorate the four-hundredth anniversary of the discovery of America, sanctioned by Congress on February 24, 1890—stirred the imagination. Despite sharp interurban competition with respect to the location of the Fair—particularly between New York and Chicago—the Exposition was accepted as a truly national celebration. The mayor of New York, for example, urged that 20,000 of his constituents attend the Fair on Manhattan Day.[124] As a public event, it was unequaled in the history of the country.

Fundamentally, however, its significance lay in the unprecedented public demonstration of civic art it inspired. This undeniably pervasive aspect of the Fair was underscored by the fact that most of the men gathered in Chicago by Daniel Burnham considered themselves essentially artists, regardless of whether their principal work was with the land, buildings, or fine arts. The noted sculptor Augustus St. Gaudens described the meeting to plan the Fair as the most impressive gathering of artists since the fifteenth century. And Charles Norton, who, in his own way, as critic and author, had traveled the same road as Olmsted, described his old friend's design contribution as essential to the needs of the nation:

> Of all American artists, Frederick Law Olmsted, who gave the
> design for the laying out of the grounds of the World's Fair,
> stands first in the production of great works which answer
> the needs and give expression to the life of our immense and
> miscellaneous democracy. The buildings which surround the
> Court of Honor, so-called, at Chicago, make a splendid display
> of monumental architecture. They show how well our
> ablest architects have studied the work of the past; and
> the arrangement of the buildings according to the general

plan produces a superb effect in the successful grouping in harmonious relations of vast and magnificent structures.[125]

From the point of view of cooperative effort, the Fair could be viewed as an outstanding example of a national social achievement. Charles Zueblin, a noted sociologist at the University of Chicago, saw the Fair in that way: "For the first time in American History," he wrote, "a complete city, equipped with all the public utilities caring for a temporary population of thousands (on one day over three quarters of a million), was built as a unit on a single architectural scale." For Zueblin, the Fair was a direct expression of Bellamy's nationalism:

The White City was the most socialistic achievement of history, the result of many minds inspired by a common aim working for the common good. . . . The individual was great but the collectivity was greater. . . . More than that, the Chicago World's Fair was a miniature of the ideal city.[126]

For Olmsted this cooperative spirit was exceeded in importance only by the atmosphere of creative freedom. The commission guiding the direction of the Exposition, he wrote,

accepted our advice, not because a majority of its members understood the grounds of it, but because they could not be led to believe that we should have given this advice without having, as experts, sound reasons for doing it. The result was due to respect for professional judgment. Comparing this experience with some in my earlier professional life, I can but think that it manifests an advance in civilization.[127]

The Fair also had other levels of social significance. Owing to Olmsted's selection of locale (Fig. 59), a section of the Chicago waterfront was protected from usurpation by the Illinois Central Railroad. The site was one of three that he and Vaux had in 1871 recommended to become part of Chicago's park system (Fig. 58). His plan for what eventually became Jackson Park had not been followed and the area remained dreary and isolated until the

Fair. When the Exposition closed, there was constructed in its place a handsome public park (Fig. 60).

In addition, the celebration could be interpreted as symbolizing the election of John Peter Altgeld as Governor of Illinois, swept into office by the second election of Grover Cleveland. Altgeld was one of the most thoroughly humane and principled men ever to hold high office in the United States; he demonstrated this by, among other acts, granting an absolute pardon to anarchists who had been unjustly convicted and sentenced after the Haymarket affair. Finally, of course, the Exposition was a brief interlude of optimism before the nation plunged into its worst economic depression up until that time.[128]

However, this was not the Fair's most enduring legacy, which was in the nature of aesthetics—style and taste—incorporated into the City Beautiful Movement of the first two decades of the twentieth century. An event that contained within it the three separate aspects of environmental planning—social, ecological, and aesthetic—was reduced essentially to a level of significance revealed only by its large ordered spaces and monumentality of design.

The failures at Chicago did not escape Olmsted. Writing to a friend who had questioned the seriousness and permanent effect of the celebration, he was bitterly frank. He denounced the influence of real-estate speculators whose sole objective in promoting the event was to delude prospective buyers into believing that the White City heralded the future. "If the lambs can be made to imagine," Olmsted wrote, "that these Exposition properties that we are making are really what they seem to be and they can be retained as permanent improvements, the wolves will be happier."[129]

Olmsted understood, too, that in a short time the entire superstructure would turn into an eyesore transformed by "natural forces [that] will warp, crack and crumble it." Hence, the underlying cultural explanation for the event was not a happy one. America had not yet progressed from its frontier mentality; it did not yet view urban and environmental planning as an important and permanent aspect of national life. Rather, the Fair reflected a state of mind "growing more or less indirectly and remotely but surely out of the frontier conditions of life from and through which our present race of Americans has been developed."[130]

The pity was that the spirit of social reform that had been rising in the last two decades of the nineteenth century—evidenced in the writings of Bellamy, Lester Ward, Thorstein Veblen, and community-oriented theorists such as Jane Addams—had no body of environmental thought on which it could draw. Olmsted had never enunciated in a major publication the broad range of goals his planning was meant to achieve. His ideas were contained within the individual reports written during the 1860's and '70's. There were other writings, but these were almost always for official bodies or published in small numbers and never widely circulated. No single document equaled, for example, his multivolume works on the antebellum South.

This was unfortunate, too, on another level. Olmsted's achievements during the second phase of his career were viewed primarily as separate and visual achievements; that is, his reputation rested primarily on the aesthetic impact of his final products rather than on the social importance of his work, the method of study and analysis that he pursued, or the interdisciplinary process through which he achieved his end. In addition to "Biltmore," Stanford University, Niagara Falls, the Columbian Exposition, and the Boston Metropolitan Park System, Olmsted made significant contributions to the environmental needs of the inner city in the form of playgrounds (Figs. 17, 66, 67) and in the preservation of urban river banks (Figs. 80–82) for ecological conservation and recreational uses. There was lacking, however, a body of literature—a school of professional thought—placing these seminal achievements into the grand perspective of an American environmental tradition. The personal tragedy of Olmsted's last years of life—loss of memory—was symbolic of the nation's larger loss—the full understanding of his total efforts.

POSTSCRIPT

Landscape architecture, or the full range of environmental considerations the term had once connoted to Olmsted and Vaux, was perpetuated in technical and aesthetic isolation from the theoretical considerations that had nurtured its early growth and development. We are, of course, grateful for the later work of men like John Nolen (1869–1937), Frederick Law Olmsted, Jr. (1870–1957), and Charles M. Robinson (1869–1917), but they did not function in the context of an integrated environmental tradition. Indeed, the full potentialities of such a tradition only became clear with the writings of Lewis Mumford and Van Wyck Brooks in the 1920's and '30's.[131]

It is not excessive at the present point in American environmental history to attempt to extrapolate some of Olmsted's principles, for surely they are at least as meaningful today as they were one hundred years ago:

1. All environmental planning includes social analysis. Implicitly or explicitly, all environmental planning and action reflects a particular view of society and the groups that compose it. It is much healthier to expose those views to open discussion than to proceed as though they do not exist.

2. Environmental planning, in order to be democratic, must be directed toward the expansion of freedom (i.e., choice) and the development of greater equality among all of the citizens of a community, particularly those who are disadvantaged.

3. Environmental planning must proceed on the assumption of the importance of cities as vital and indispensable centers of culture and civilization. Planning that views cities as separate from regions or unrelated to considerations of ecology and community cannot hope to succeed.

4. All environmental planning must proceed in the awareness that any alteration of nature—no matter how small—has deep implications for the ecological processes of the immediate area and the larger region.

5. Environmental planning is a team effort involving the co-operation of representatives of the natural and social sciences and their allied disciplines of architecture, engineering, and landscape architecture.

6. The intrusion of politics at the professional and technical level can only disrupt sound environmental planning. Once having established by close "user" involvement the goals of the plan, the actual execution of the project is a matter of expert—not lay—opinion. A review of the final product—the constant evaluation of the plan's effect—is, however, a matter of equal importance to both users and professionals.

7. The maintenance and preservation of completed projects and the periodic review of their social, ecological, and aesthetic effects is as vital for the public good as the original plan itself. Indeed, a project, no matter how well planned, can easily become a focal point for social distress if maintenance and preservation are not given the highest priority. Completed projects that are not viewed as part of the environment, to be continuously studied, are doomed to become dead monuments.

8. And finally, all environmental planning must be thought of in historic context. To plan without relationship to past efforts, achievements, and failures is to display an arrogance and mindlessness that can only result in costly errors and countless lost opportunities. The present condition of most of Olmsted's works—particularly his urban parks—is symptomatic of the extent to which environmental planning is ignored today. The challenge in environmental planning and design remains sociological, ecological, and aesthetic, as in Olmsted's day. Thus, it would be salutary on many levels of national well-being if the highest priority were given to the restoration and maintenance of all his landscape monuments and to the establishment of sound procedures for their daily use. This would demonstrate that we truly mean to extend to our larger environments the scientific and social planning Olmsted began.

ILLUSTRATIONS

These illustrations have been selected and arranged so as to form a visual essay which, although related to the text, can be studied independently from it. They offer examples of most of the types and scales of the projects for which Frederick Law Olmsted, Sr. was responsible and depict as well some of the scientific, social, aesthetic, and technical aspects of his planning and design.

2. New York City, Air View of Central Park. "Everything invites to the arts of agriculture, of gardening, and domestic architecture." (Emerson)

3. Chicago, World's Columbian Exposition, Aerial View (1893). That Olmsted had great respect for Burnham's organizational ability is clear from this conclusion: "Too high an estimate cannot be placed on the industry, skill and tact with which this result [World's Fair] was secured by the master of us all . . . Mr. [Daniel H.] Burnham." (See Fig. 59.)

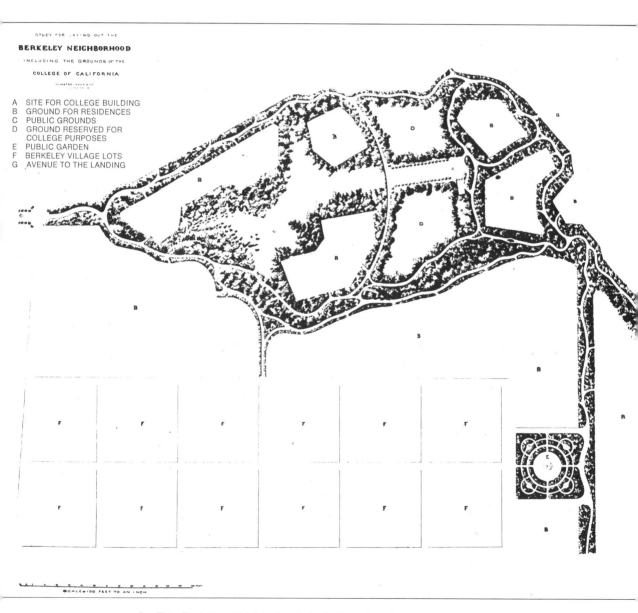

4. The Berkeley Neighborhood Including the Grounds of the College of California, 1866, Olmsted, Vaux & Co., Landscape Architects. This campus plan demonstrates Olmsted's early insistence on a small-scaled, flexible design of land. In addition, it reflects his adaptation of "a picturesque, rather than a formal and perfectly symmetrical arrangement." The picturesque was an aesthetic of land manipulation that originated in England in the early part of the eighteenth century.

5. The Leland Stanford Junior University, Palo Alto, California—Plan of Central Premises, 1888, Shepley, Rutan & Coolidge, Architects; F. L. Olmsted and J. C. Olmsted, Landscape Architects. "The central buildings of the University are to stand in the midst of the plain. This has been determined by the founders chiefly in order that no topographical difficulties need ever stand in the way of setting other buildings as they may in the future, one after another, be found desirable, in eligible, orderly and symmetrical relation and connection with those earlier provided."

6. Central Park, New York City. View of Mt. Prospect Looking Eastward, ca. 1860. Lithograph of Ferd Mayer & Co., N. Y., Drawn from Nature by A. Ribstein. Almost all of the views of Central Park were designed as an antithesis to the city—the views being either to the park itself or, as in this lithograph, to the horizon.

7. Central Park: Entrance at Corner of Eighth Avenue and Fifty-ninth Street, 1863, R. M. Hunt, Architect.

8. Central Park: Seventh Avenue Entrance on Fifty-ninth Street, 1863, R. M. Hunt, Architect. "The various designs for the several gates, it will be seen, are all of a monumental character. . . . If they are carried out with becoming taste and skill, we may look forward to having such a *facade*, if we may call it so, to our grand pleasure ground as no city in the world can boast of."

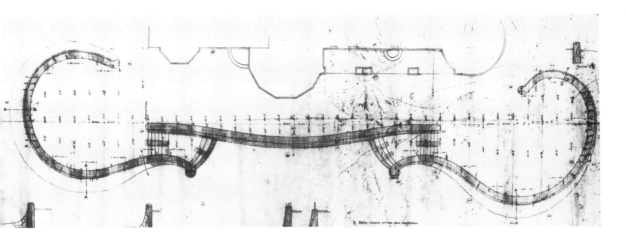

9. Plan of Terrace, House for Mrs. Robert Treat Paine, Waltham, Massachusetts, 1886. Paine (1835–1910), a Boston philanthropist, was a great-grandson of Robert Treat Paine, a signer of the Declaration of Independence.

10. Paine Terrace, ca. 1890.

11. Paine Terrace, ca. 1935.

12. Oakes Ames Memorial Hall, North Easton, Massachusetts, 1879–81, H. H. Richardson, Architect; F. L. Olmsted, Landscape Architect.

13. F. L. Ames Gate Lodge, North Easton. Exterior from southwest 1880–81, H. H. Richardson, Architect; F. L. Olmsted, Landscape Architect.

14. Boston and Albany Railroad Station at North Easton, Massachusetts, 1882, H. H. Richardson, Architect; F. L. Olmsted, Landscape Architect.

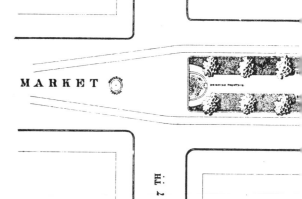

15.   Sketch of Arbor, Logan Place, Louisville, 1892.

16.   Plan of Logan Place, Louisville, 1892, F. L. Olmsted & Co., Landscape Architects; Emil Mahlo, Park Engineer.

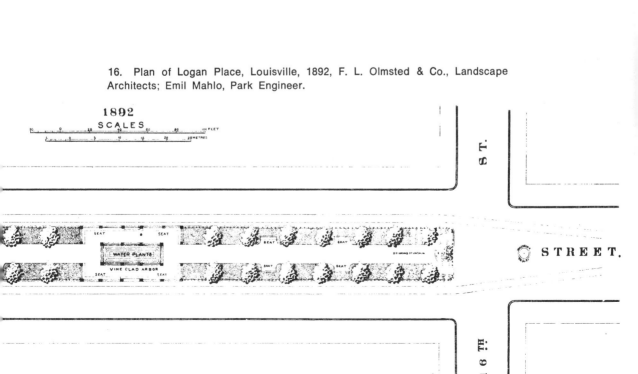

CITY OF BOSTON — PARK DEPARTMENT
THOMAS L. LIVERMORE, FRANCIS A. WALKER, PAUL H. KENDRICKEN, COMMISSIONERS.

PLAN OF
CHARLESBANK
—1892—

SCALES

WILLIAM JACKSON
CITY ENGINEER

F. L. OLMSTED & CO., LANDSCAPE ARCHITECTS
DECEMBER 1892

17.   Plan of Charlesbank, Boston, 1892, F. L. Olmsted & Co., Landscape Architects; William Jackson, City Engineer. "[The facilities of Charlesbank] were suggested and planned in all their minutest details by Mr. Frederick Law Olmsted, in accordance with his steadfast aim to make the public parks administer to all possible open-air recreative uses by the largest number of people." These facilities included areas for a variety of outdoor recreational sports such as gymnastics and quoits in spaces planned for different age groups.

18.   Revised Study of a Plan for Marine Park, Boston, December 1889, F. L. and J. C. Olmsted, Landscape Architects. "Its simple, but remarkable[,] ingenious, plan utilizes for recreative purposes in the fullest possible way the advantages of the site, both natural and suggested by its fortunate location—boating, sailing, bathing, and the enjoyment of sea air and the varied spectacle of the maritime life of the harbor and bay."

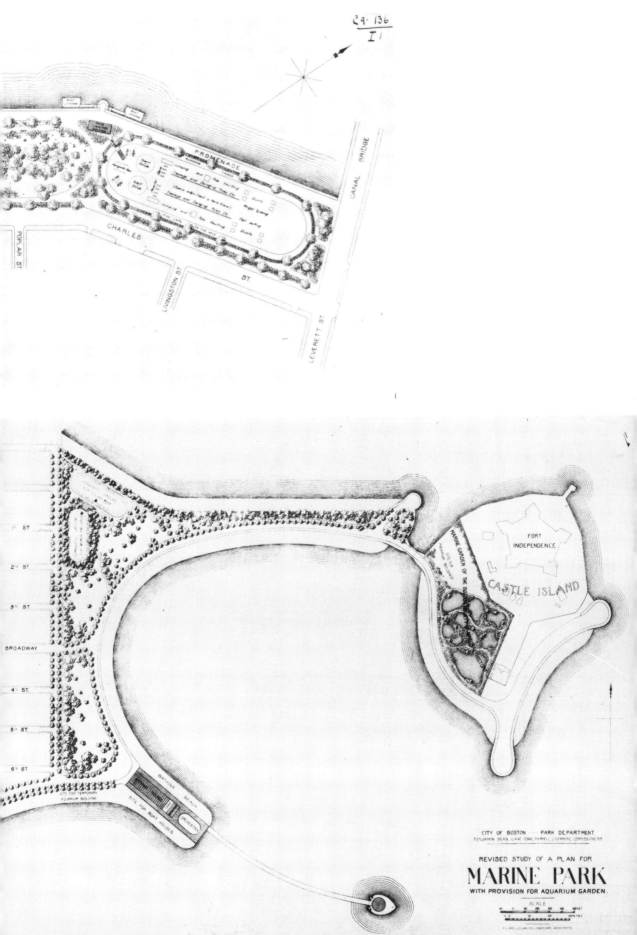

PROMENADE

POPLAR ST

CHARLES

LIVINGSTON ST

ST

LEVERETT ST

CANAL BRIDGE

1ˢᵗ ST

2ᴺᴰ ST

3ᴿᴰ ST

BROADWAY

4ᵀᴴ ST

5ᵀᴴ ST

6ᵀᴴ ST

FORT
INDEPENDENCE

CASTLE ISLAND

BATHING BEACH

SITE FOR BOAT HOUSES

CITY OF BOSTON — PARK DEPARTMENT

REVISED STUDY OF A PLAN FOR

MARINE PARK

WITH PROVISION FOR AQUARIUM GARDEN.

SCALE

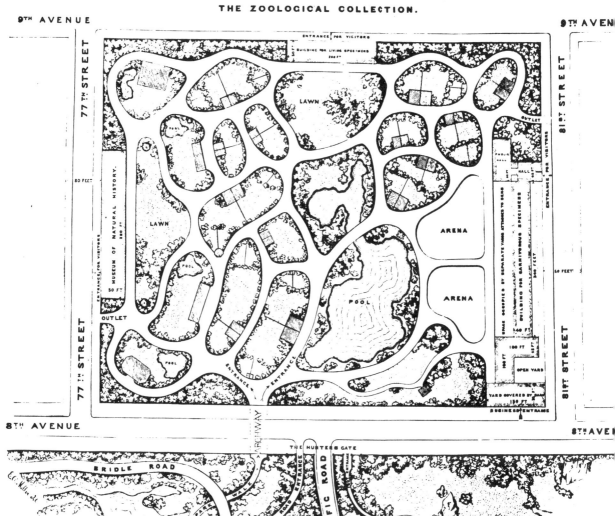

19. Proposed Plan for the Zoological Collection (later site for the American Museum of Natural History), New York City, 1866, by Olmsted, Vaux & Co., Landscape Architects.

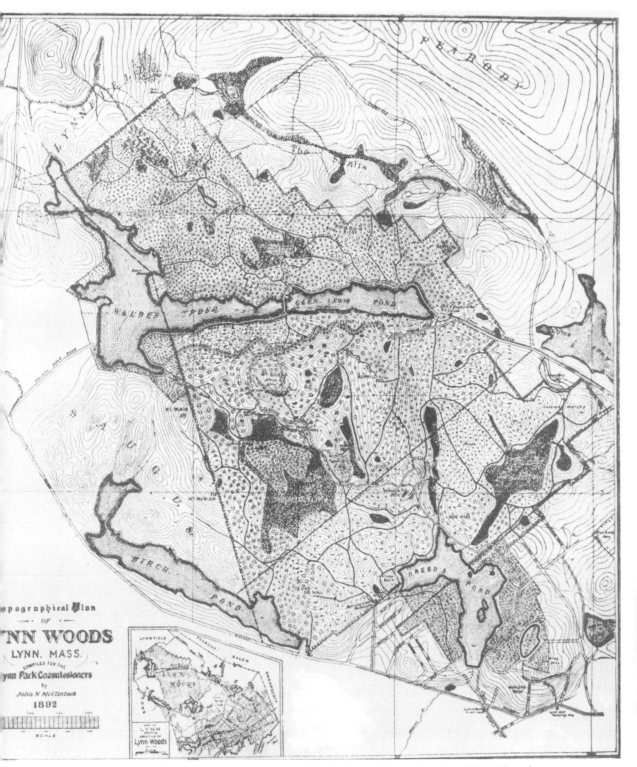

20. Topographical Plan of Lynn Woods, Lynn, Massachusetts, 1892. Although Olmsted's proposal in 1889 for Lynn Woods was for a recreational area, the objective of conservation of natural resources was equally important, as the Park Commissioners of Lynn wrote in their *Second Annual Report:* "The preservation of forests is becoming a question of vital interest to the whole country. The destruction of timber in the mountainous regions that make the watershed of our great rivers, has aroused the public mind to consider the consequences. In our small field we may show a public spirit and bestow a care upon the forests around us that may be a healthful example."

GENERAL PLAN
OF
RIVERSIDE

OLMSTED, VAUX & CO. LANDSCAPE ARCHITECTS

1869.

CHICAGO LITHOGRAPHING CO. CHICAGO.

Scale 400 feet to an inch.

21. General Plan of Riverside, Illinois, 1869, Olmsted, Vaux & Co., Landscape Architects. The planners' chief physical goal in this design was, after incorporating the railroad as the principal means of transportation to Chicago and projecting a parkway as an alternate means for recreational travel to the city, to maximize the site's chief topographical feature, the Des Plaines river.

The social objectives of the plan were twofold: to encourage as much communal spirit as possible by providing maximum functional, attractive public space and by preventing private construction from intruding on public functions and forms. A guiding principle of this social design was the subdivision of the site into small "villagelike" areas, each in proximity to "public grounds . . . [having] the character of informal village greens, commons and playgrounds." The villages were linked into one community by public drives and walks, with their recreational uses.

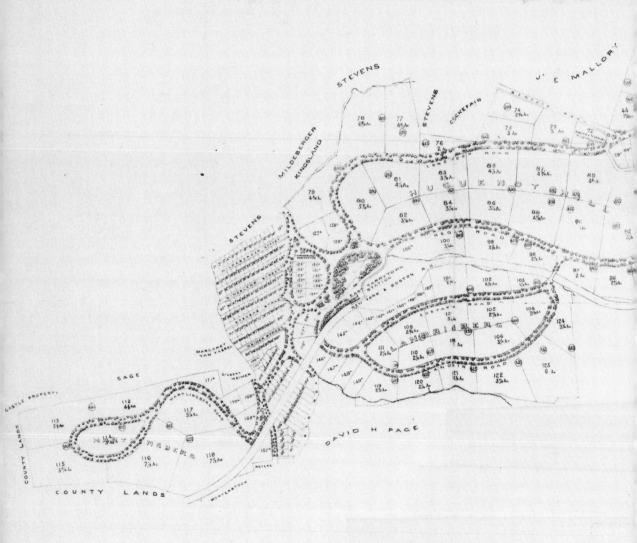

TARRYTOWN HEIGHTS LAND COMPANY

PLAN OF THE LAND

BELONGING TO THE COMPANY

AS LAID OUT BY

OLMSTED VAUX & CO LANDSCAPE ARCHITECTS

1871

22. Tarrytown Heights Land Company, New York, Plan of the Land, 1871, Olmsted, Vaux & Co., Landscape Architects. The principal heights and valleys in the villa districts are distinguished by names (as Carlsberg, Elzendale, etc.) in large open letters; each villa lot is numbered and its size given in acres: $\frac{159}{63/6}$ Ac; the elevation above low water level of the Hudson at Tarrytown, of the highest ground in each villa lot, is shown by figures in a circle: (515); the village lots are numbered in two series: 1ᵃ to 171ᵃ and 1ᵇ to 69ᵇ.

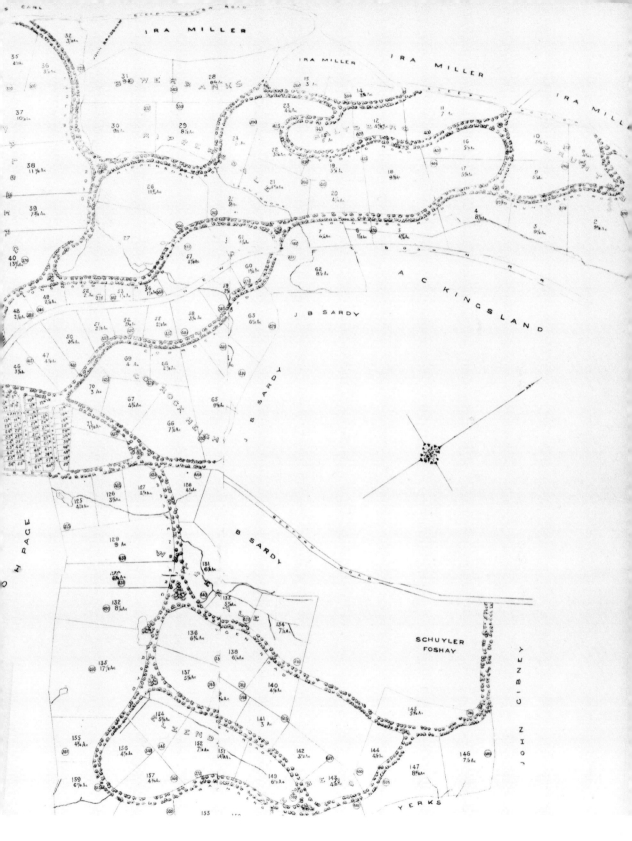

23. Columbia Institution for the Deaf and Dumb (Gallaudet College), Washington, D.C., 1866, Olmsted, Vaux & Co., Landscape Architects. "In a well-regulated garden the senses of sight and smell are gratified in a most complete and innocent way, and there seems, indeed, to be no reason why the studies of horticulture, botany, ornamental gardening, and rural architecture should not be pursued to great advantage by your students if proper facilities are offered at the outset, and due importance is attached to that influential automatic education which depends entirely upon an habitual daily contemplation of good examples."

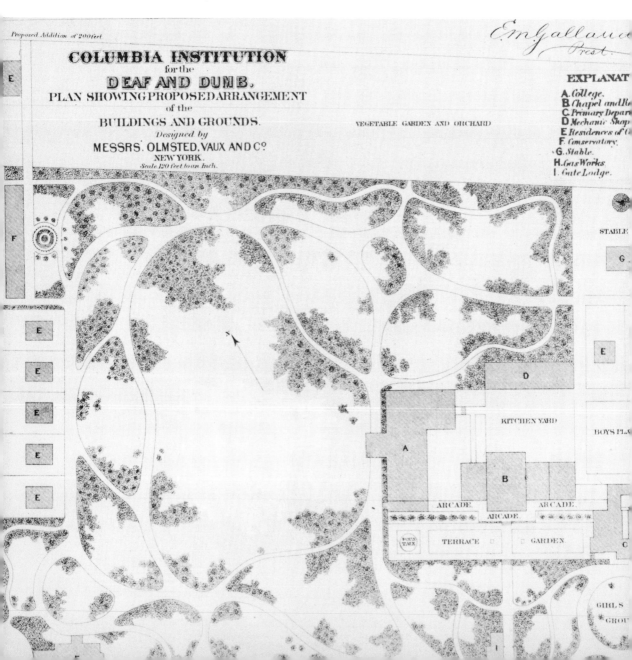

24. Mountain View Cemetery, Oakland, California, 1865. "A part of your ground is a plain surface, mainly level. It is as far as possible, therefore, from being suggestive of picturesque treatment. You will observe, that in the portion of the plan which I offer you covering this part of the ground, each road is carried from one end to the other in a straight line, and bordered by rows of trees forming an avenue. This is, under the circumstances, the simplest and most natural course."

25. Buffalo, New York, State Hospital, Administration Building, H. H. Richardson, Architect; F. L. Olmsted, Landscape Architect. Plans presented 1870–72; Olmsted collaborated on the siting of the building and on the design of the grounds (1871), which border Delaware Park (See Fig. 52).

26. Albany, New York, State Capitol, 1875–76, H. H. Richardson and Leopold Eidlitz, Architects; F. L. Olmsted, Landscape Architect. Olmsted was involved in all aspects of the effort to complete the design for this very costly and controversial structure. His advice was incorporated by the two architects with whom he collaborated. He was, in fact, the chief author of the 1876 report explaining and defending the architects' plan, the goal of which was "that the Capitol shall be an architectural monument worthy of the grandeur of the Empire State."

27. Biltmore, North Carolina, George W. Vanderbilt Estate, ca. 1890.

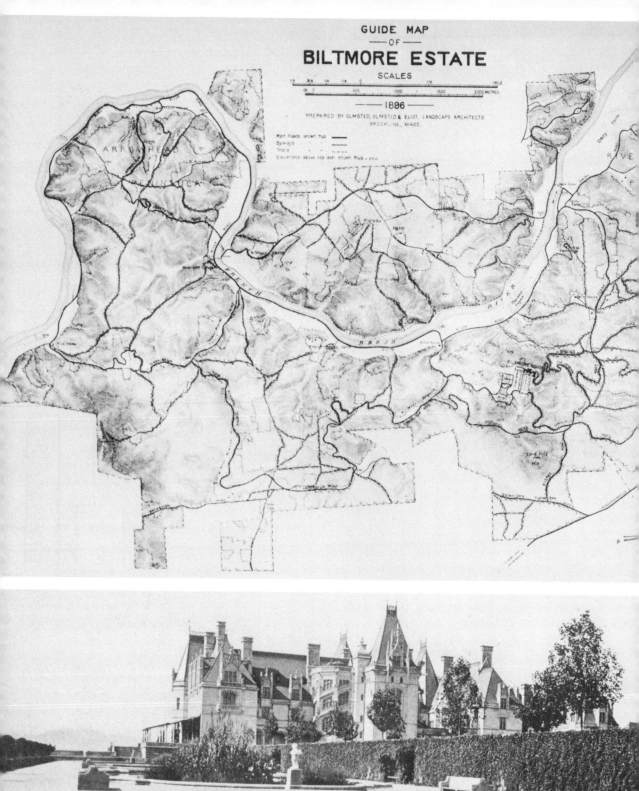

GUIDE MAP
OF
BILTMORE ESTATE
SCALES

1896

PREPARED BY OLMSTED, OLMSTED & ELIOT, LANDSCAPE ARCHITECTS
BROOKLINE, MASS.

Main Roads shown thus
Byways
Trails
Elevations above sea level shown thus

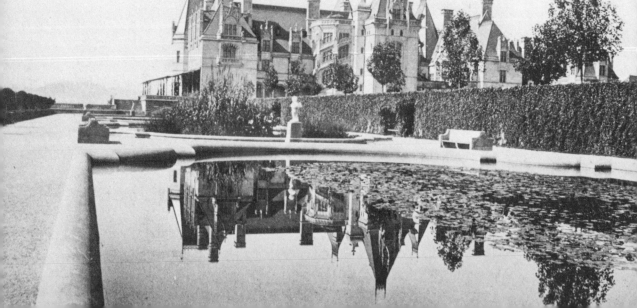

28. Asheville, North Carolina, Guide Map of Biltmore Estate, 1896, Olmsted, Olmsted & Eliot, Landscape Architects. "I want you to recognize . . . that the ruling interest of the estate is not . . . agricultural; it is not landscape gardening; it is simply *industrial forestry;* the management of trees with reference to commercial profit."

29. Biltmore, North Carolina, R. M. Hunt, Architect, 1888–95; F. L. Olmsted, Landscape Architect, 1888–95.

30. "The Domes of the Yosemite," by Albert Bierstadt. "The first point to be kept in mind then is the preservation and maintenance as exactly as is possible of the natural scenery."

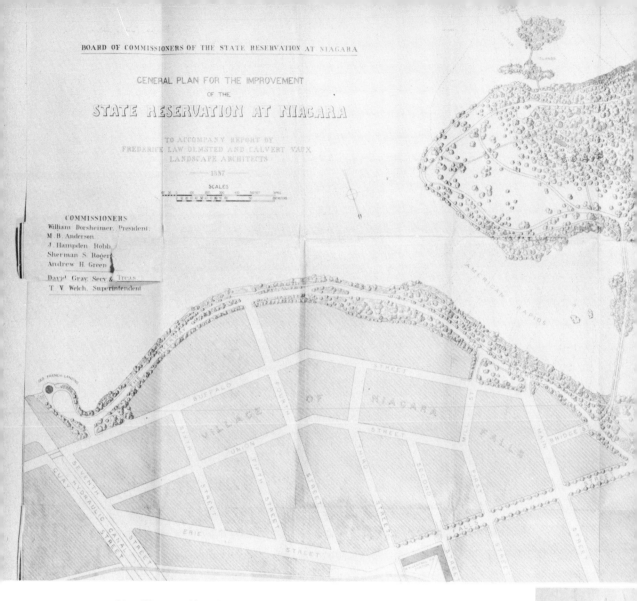

31. Niagara, New York, General Plan for the Improvement of the State Reservation at Niagara, 1887, F. L. Olmsted and C. Vaux, Landscape Architects. The objective of the plan was preventive as well as remedial; the dilapidated buildings and commercial structures removed were merely indications of what would happen to the Falls as the need for sources of industrial energy increased. Hence, the goal was to preserve what surely would be lost. As Olmsted wrote: "[to provide] as amply as practicable for great throngs of people . . . to preserve and develop a particular character of natural scenery on a great scale avoiding as much as possible all manifestation of art, human labor, or human purpose." Goat Island is to the right.

32. Boston Park System: From Commons to Franklin Park, 1896, Olmsted, Olmsted & Eliot, Landscape Architects. "The main distinctive characteristic of the Boston municipal system is its design as a series of parks, each possessing an individual landscape character and special recreative functions, united by a chain of drives, rides and walks, forming a grand parkway of picturesque type five miles in extent, reaching from the heart of the city into the rural scenery of the suburbs."

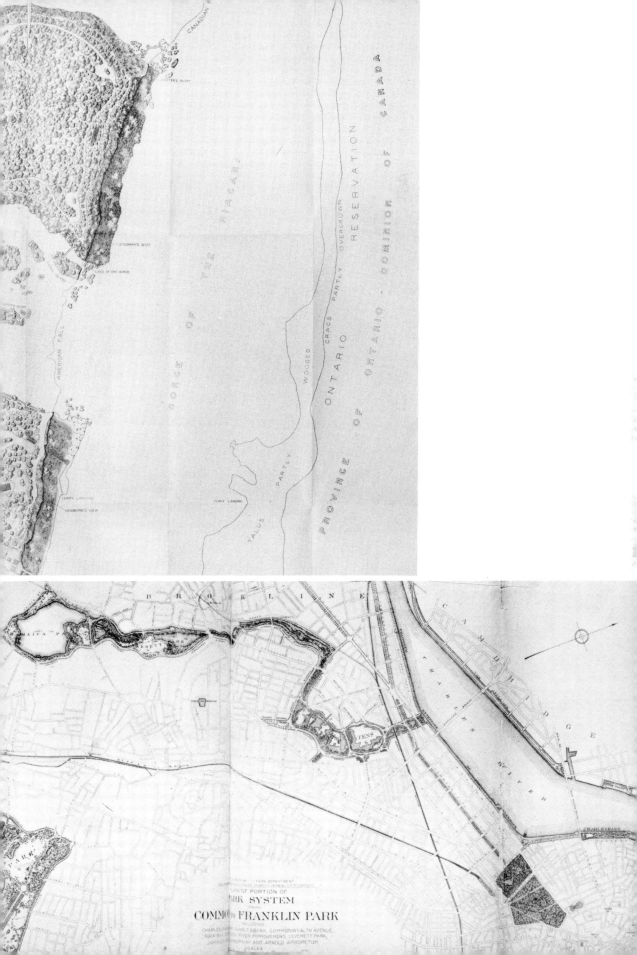

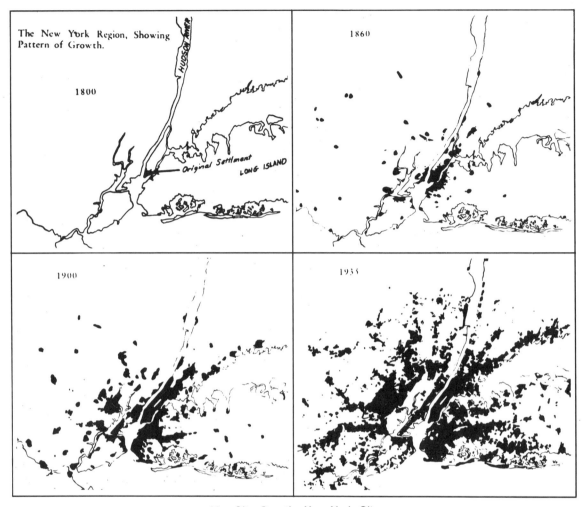

The New York Region, Showing Pattern of Growth.

1800

HUDSON RIVER

Original Settlement

LONG ISLAND

1860

1900

1935

33.   City Growth: New York City.

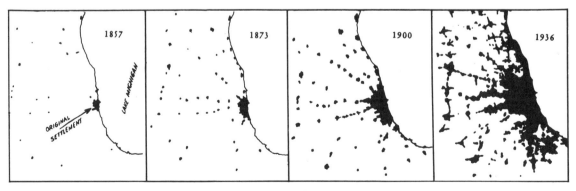

1857

ORIGINAL SETTLEMENT

LAKE MICHIGAN

1873

1900

1936

34.   City Growth: The Chicago Region.

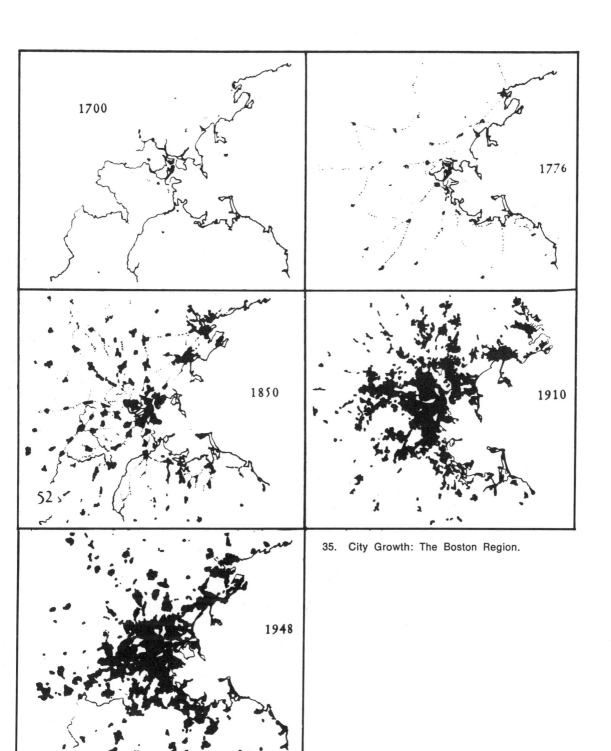

1700

1776

1850

52

1910

1948

35. City Growth: The Boston Region.

IV OLMSTED AND THE PLANNING OF CITIES

Boston

36. View of Boston, July 4, 1870.

37. Boston, Map of Boston and a Part of Its Suburbs, Showing Public Recreation Grounds, 1886. "There has been established within the past two years, a very important and extensive system of metropolitan parks for the benefit of the cluster of municipalities known as 'Greater Boston' and organized for this purpose as the Metropolitan Parks District. This district comprises thirty-seven municipalities."

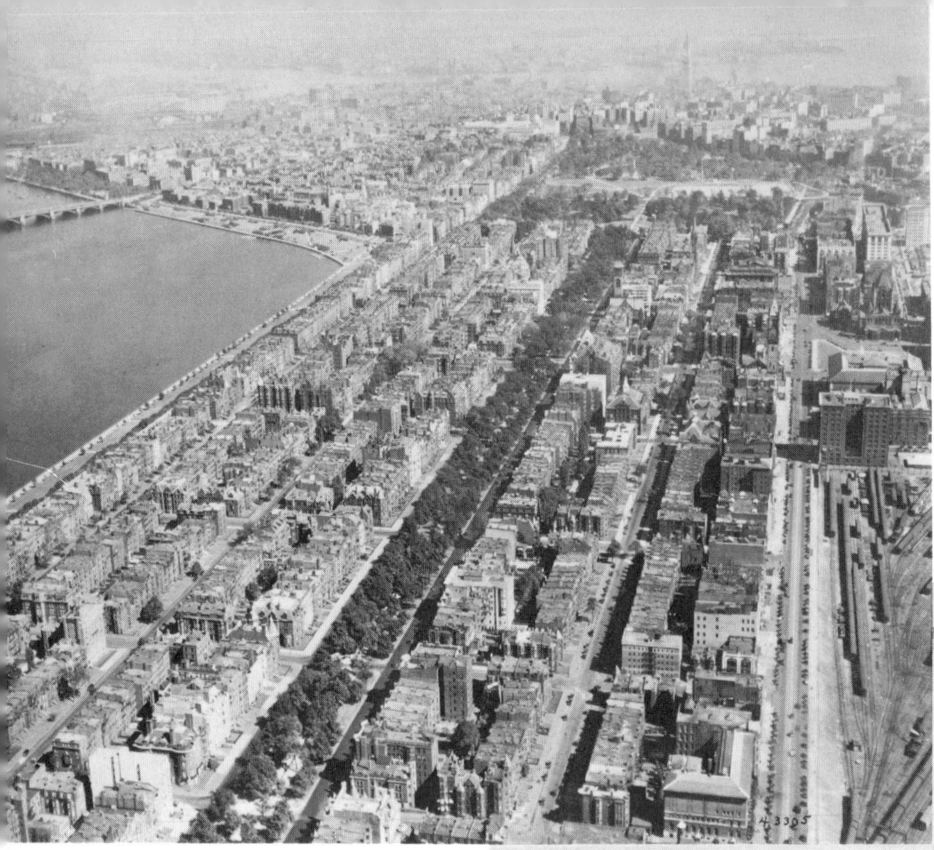

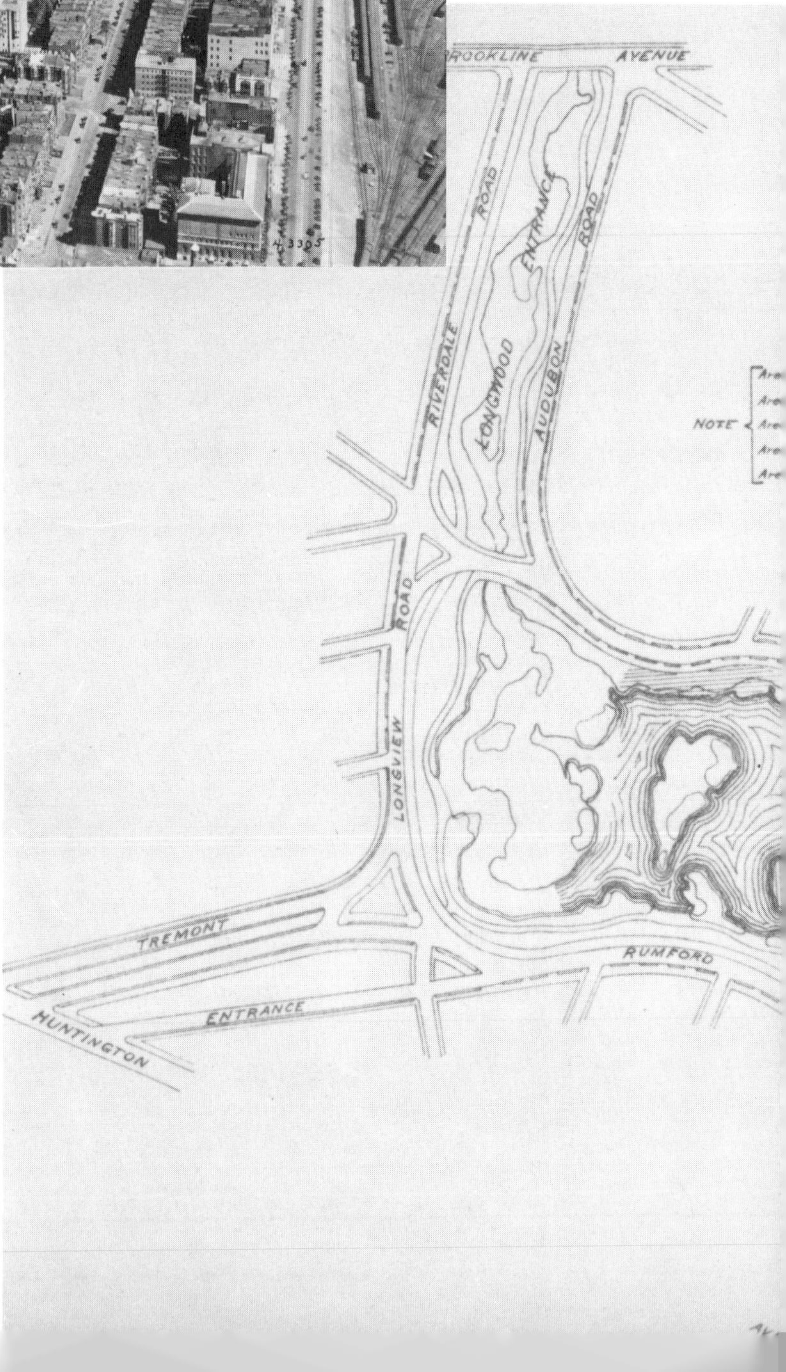

BROOKLINE
AVENUE
RIVERDALE
ROAD
LONGWOOD
ENTRANCE
AUDUBON
ROAD
NOTE
LONGVIEW
ROAD
TREMONT
MUNTINGTON
ENTRANCE
RUMFORD

38. Boston, Back Bay, 1925 (Commonwealth Avenue section). Olmsted's planning incorporated the formalism of the Back Bay, lending a unity to that area and integrating it within the Boston Park System. "Turf, trees, water, and other natural objects unnaturally arranged, but not in the main unpleasingly in consideration of the stately rows of buildings and other architectural and artificial objects with which they must stand associated, and the necessary thoroughfares passing among them."

39. Improvement of Back Bay (Fenway section) Showing Progress of Portions of Work, to December 31, 1885, F. L. Olmsted, Landscape Architect; William Jackson, City Engineer. "The leading and only justifying purpose of the Back Bay Improvement, under the present design, is the abatement of a complicated nuisance, threatening soon to be a deadly peril to the whole city as a propagating and breeding-ground of pestilential epidemics."

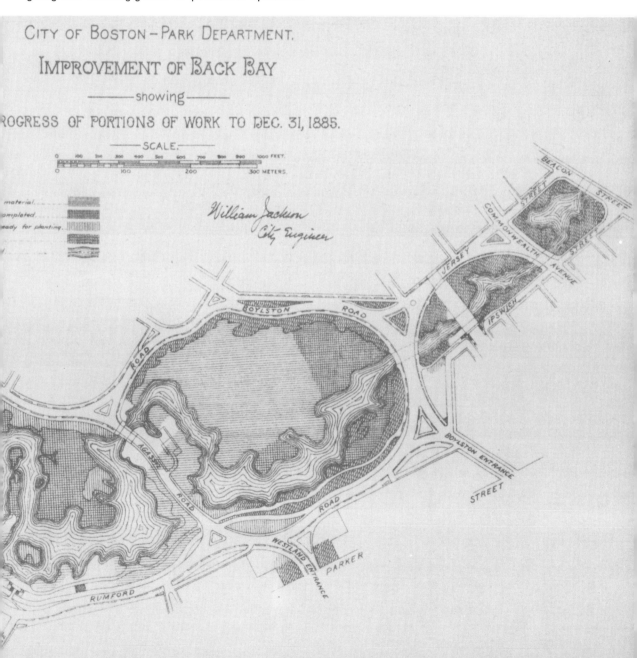

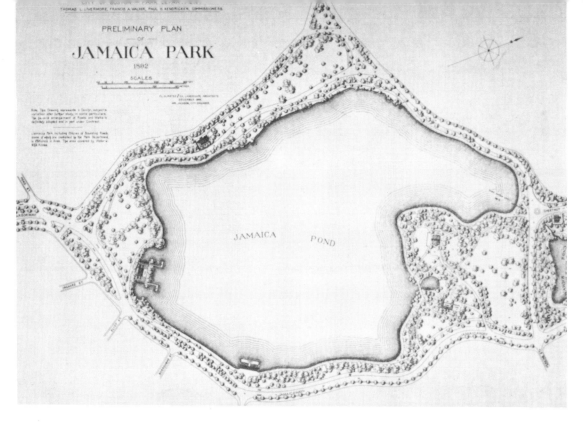

40. Preliminary plan of Jamaica Park, Boston, December 1892, F. L. Olmsted & Co., Landscape Architects; William Jackson, City Engineer.

41. Map of Proposed Arnold Arboretum, Boston, 1879, F. L. Olmsted, Landscape Architect.

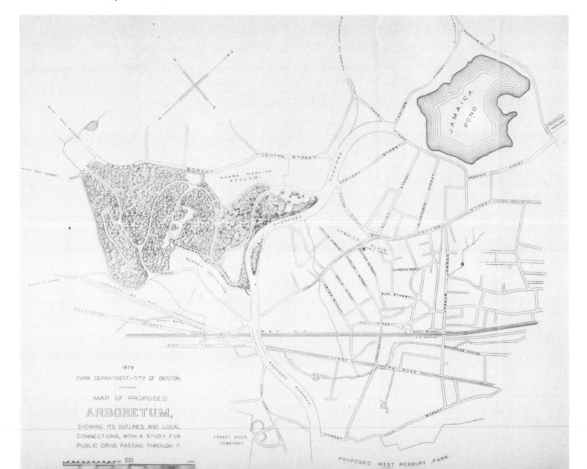

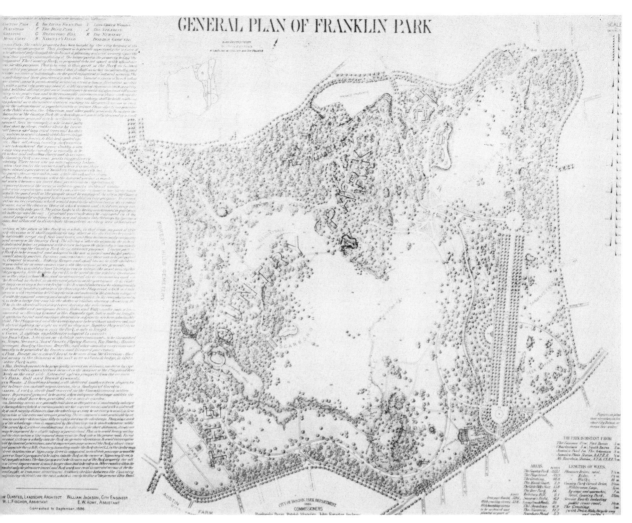

42. General Plan of Franklin Park, Boston, 1885. Corrected to 1896. "Complete escape from the town." Franklin Park was meant to serve Boston as Central Park was meant to serve New York City and Prospect Park the City of Brooklyn—as a "natural" environment within an urban community (See Figs. 97, 105).

43. Revised Preliminary Plan of Wood Island Park, Boston, September 25, 1891, F. L. Olmsted & Co., Landscape Architects; William Jackson, City Engineer. "Wood Island Park is a local pleasure-ground for East Boston. . . . The greater portion of the space is devoted to playground and gymnastic purposes."

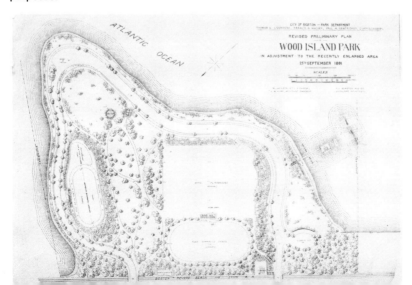

44. Preliminary Plan of Beardsley Park, 1884, F. L. and J. C. Olmsted, Landscape Architects. "The want of Bridgeport is a simple, rural park."

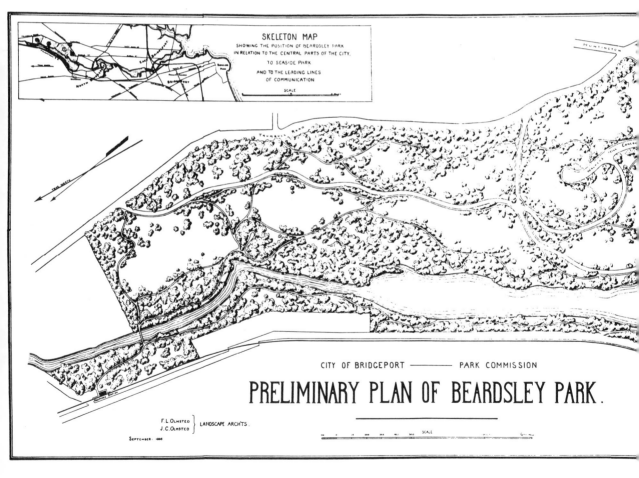

45. Map of the cities of New York, Brooklyn, Jersey City, Hudson City, and Hoboken, 1859, prepared by M. Driggs. This 1859 map portrays Brooklyn as part of a larger metropolitan area, as Olmsted did when he wrote "we regard Brooklyn as an integral part of what today is the metropolis of the nation." Olmsted believed that planners had to deal with the real social and economic forces of urban growth and change —not artificial political boundaries.

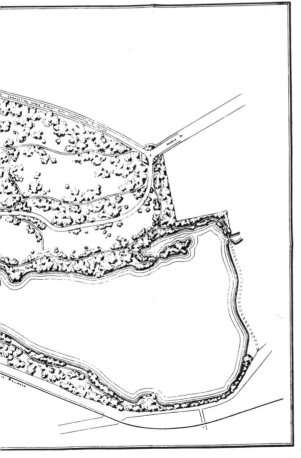

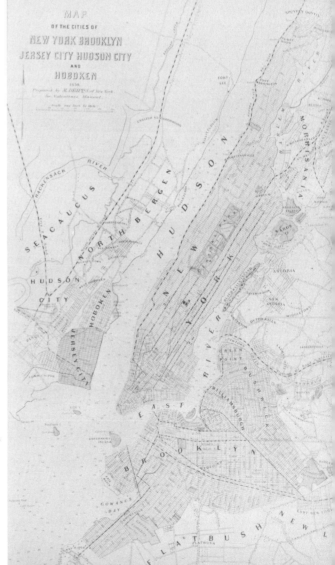

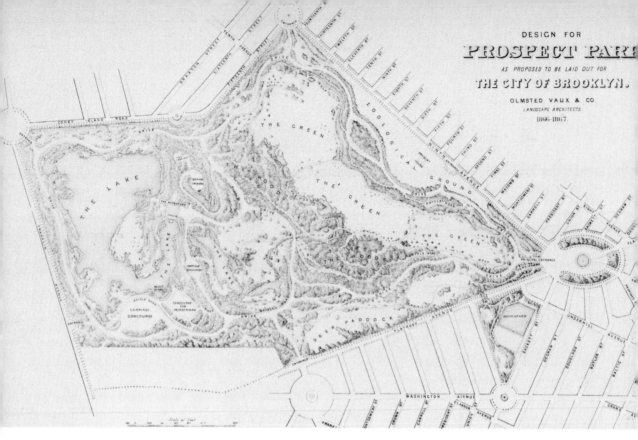

46. Proposed Design for Prospect Park, Brooklyn, 1866–67, Olmsted, Vaux & Co., Landscape Architects. Prospect Park was the second of the large "country-like" parks planned by Olmsted and Vaux for a major urban center. As with many of Olmsted's projects, it can be understood on multiple levels: scientific, technological, social, economic, political, and aesthetic. Its fundamental social significance was as a large, ordered area that complemented and strengthened the city by making available to all of its citizens a space that was antithetical to the commercial city. The park was meant to be an example of a public recreation area, scientifically planned and managed, constructed with natural materials and in terms of a natural aesthetic.

47. Plan for Parade Ground, Brooklyn, 1867, Olmsted, Vaux & Co., Landscape Architects. American cities, during most of the nineteenth century, required specialized places for reviews of military parades. The Civil War led to the heightened importance of local military units, to their continuous training, and to their participation in celebrations of all kinds. The Parade Ground was designed as a place for the training of troops and for the public review of such activities (Compare Fig. 54).

48. Design for Fort Green[e] or Washington Park, Brooklyn, 1867, Olmsted, Vaux & Co. Fort Greene Park was one of several neighborhood parks in Brooklyn designed by Olmstead and Vaux. It is important for having incorporated several different functions: (1) civic meetings were held there: nineteenth-century American cities required open spaces for large audiences, particularly at election time, or during national holidays, such as the Fourth of July; (2) the park and its principal architectural structure were renamed to commemorate the role of Brooklyn in the Revolutionary War; and (3) it was a public space for outdoor recreation in what was in 1867, by American standards, a dense residential area.

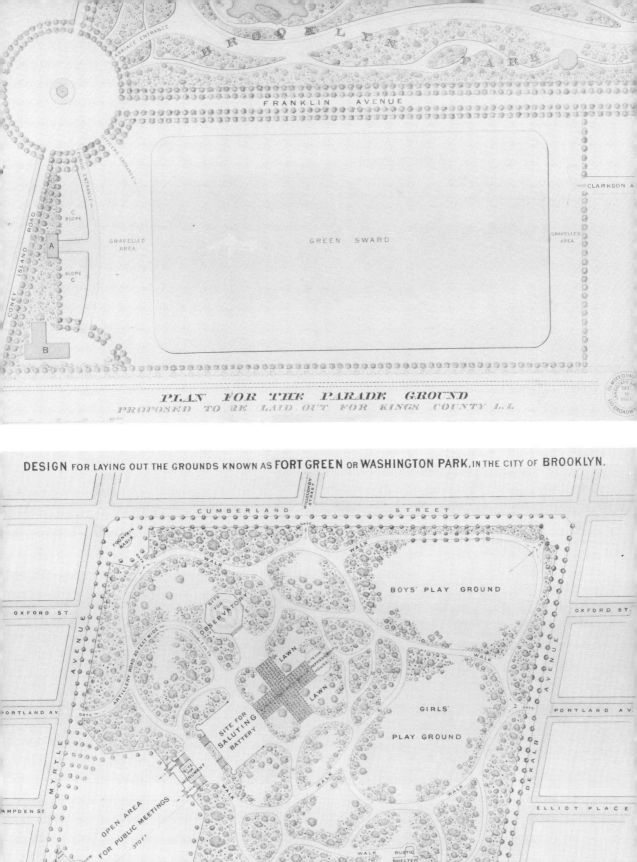

PLAN FOR THE PARADE GROUND
PROPOSED TO BE LAID OUT FOR KINGS COUNTY L.I.

BROOKLYN PARK

FRANKLIN AVENUE

CARRIAGE ENTRANCE

PUBLIC ENTRANCE

CONEY ISLAND ROAD

C SLOPE

A

SLOPE C

B

GRAVELLED AREA

GREEN SWARD

GRAVELLED AREA

CLARKSON A

DESIGN FOR LAYING OUT THE GROUNDS KNOWN AS **FORT GREEN** OR **WASHINGTON PARK**, IN THE CITY OF **BROOKLYN.**

CUMBERLAND STREET

WILLOUGHBY STREET

FOUNTAIN BASIN

WALK

GATE

WALK

BOYS' PLAY GROUND

OXFORD ST.

OXFORD ST.

SITE FOR OBSERVATORY

ARTILLERY ROAD 80 FEET WIDE

LAWN

LAWN

WALK

GIRLS'

PORTLAND AV.

PORTLAND AV.

MYRTLE AVENUE

GATE

SITE FOR SALUTING BATTERY

MONUMENT

PLAY GROUND

DEKALB AVENUE

CAMPDEN ST.

WALK

GATE

WALK

ELLIOT PLACE

OPEN AREA FOR PUBLIC MEETINGS

370 FT

WALK

RUSTIC SHELTER

CANTON STREET

WILLOUGHBY STREET

BOLIVAR ST.

GATE

WALK

GATE

FORT GREEN PLACE

MODIFICATION PROPOSED LINE OF PRESENT BOUNDARY FENCE MODIFICATION PROPOSED

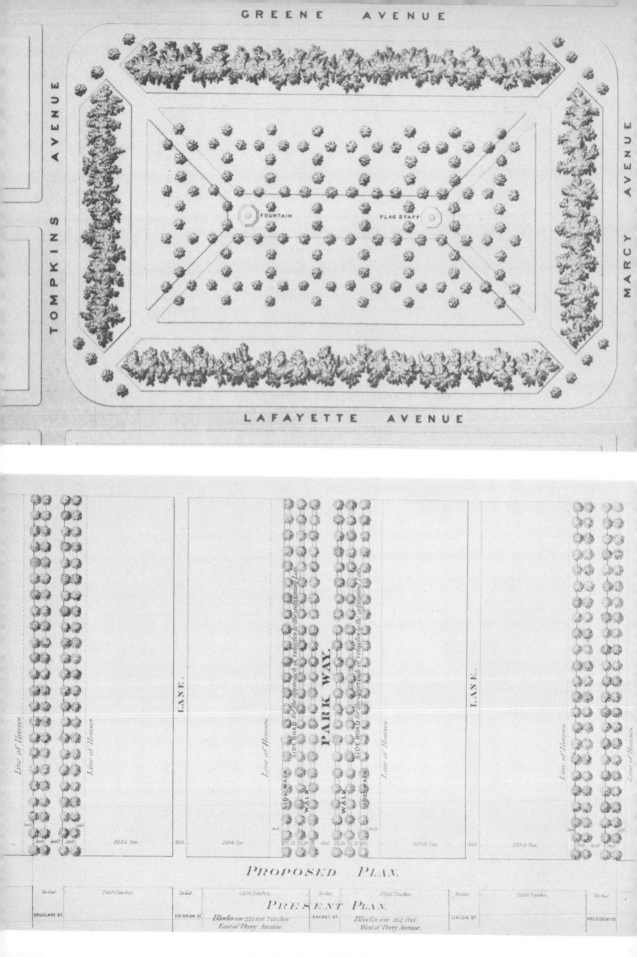

49. Design for Laying Out Tompkins Park, Brooklyn, 1871, Olmsted, Vaux & Co. Tompkins Park is a good example of an early Olmsted and Vaux design for a small urban open space in a residential area. It was intended as a seating area for neighborhood residents, particularly mothers and small children out for an afternoon stroll. The walks are laid out so as not to impede pedestrian through-traffic.

50. Plan of a proposed portion of Eastern Parkway, Brooklyn, 1868, Olmsted, Vaux & Co. The parkway, which was patterned after the Boulevard De L'Impératrice, designed for Paris under the direction of Baron Haussmann, provided an alternative environment to the commercial street. Except for delivery vehicles and domestic carriages, this wide tree-lined parkway was designed for walking and sitting. In later years, bicycle riding would be planned for on the parkways.

Buffalo, New York

51. Olmsted's Sketch Map of Buffalo, 1876, F. L. Olmsted. "Buffalo is forming the most complete system of recreation-grounds of any city in the United States."

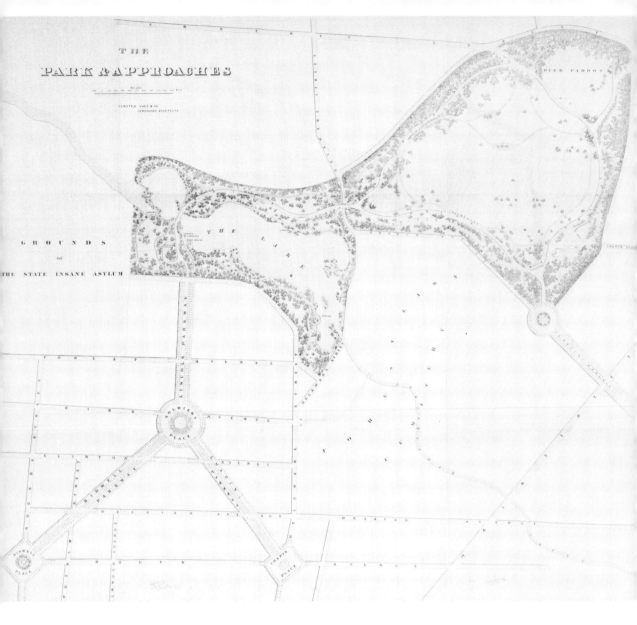

52. [Delaware] Park and Approaches, Buffalo, 1868, Olmsted, Vaux & Co.,
Landscape Architects. Delaware Park was designed to serve the city of Buffalo as Central Park was designed to meet the open-space needs of New York
City. However, it was planned as part of an integrated parks-parkway system,
as was Prospect Park in Brooklyn. Note that on the grounds of the State
Insane Asylum was to be located the Buffalo State Hospital Building, later
designed by H. H. Richardson (See Figs. 25, 104).

53. The Front, Buffalo, 1868, Olmsted, Vaux & Co., Landscape Architects.

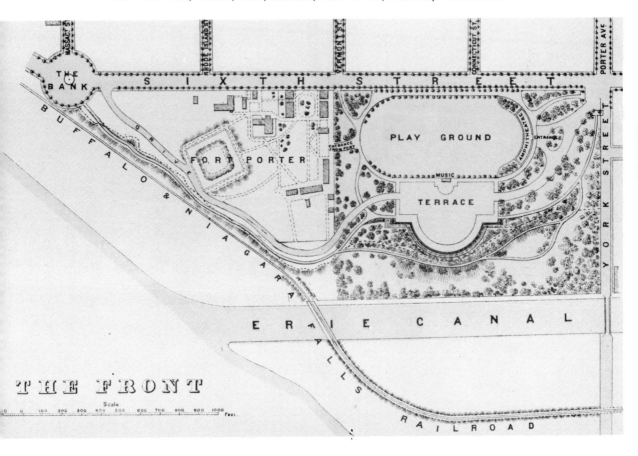

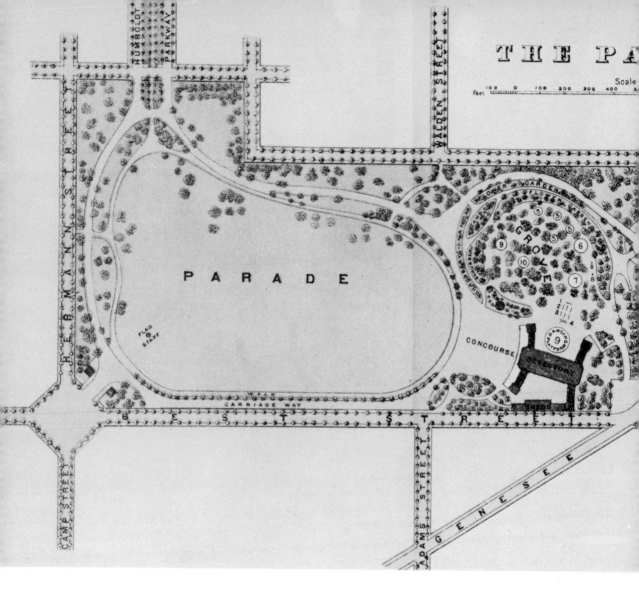

THE PA[RK]

Scale

Feet   100 0   100   200 300 400

WALDEN STREET

HUMBOLDT PARKWAY

HERMANN STREET

PARADE

FLAG STAFF

WALK
CARRIAGE WAY

BEST   STREET

CAMP STREET

ADAMS STREET

GENESEE

FLOWER GARDEN

GROVE

5 5 5
5 5
9   6
10   8 8
7
1
2
3

CONCOURSE

DANCING PLATFORM
9

REFECTORY

SHEDS

54. The Parade, Buffalo, 1868, Olmsted, Vaux & Co., Landscape Architects.

55. Study Plan for Improvement of Niagara Square, Buffalo, October 1874, F. L. Olmsted, Landscape Architect.

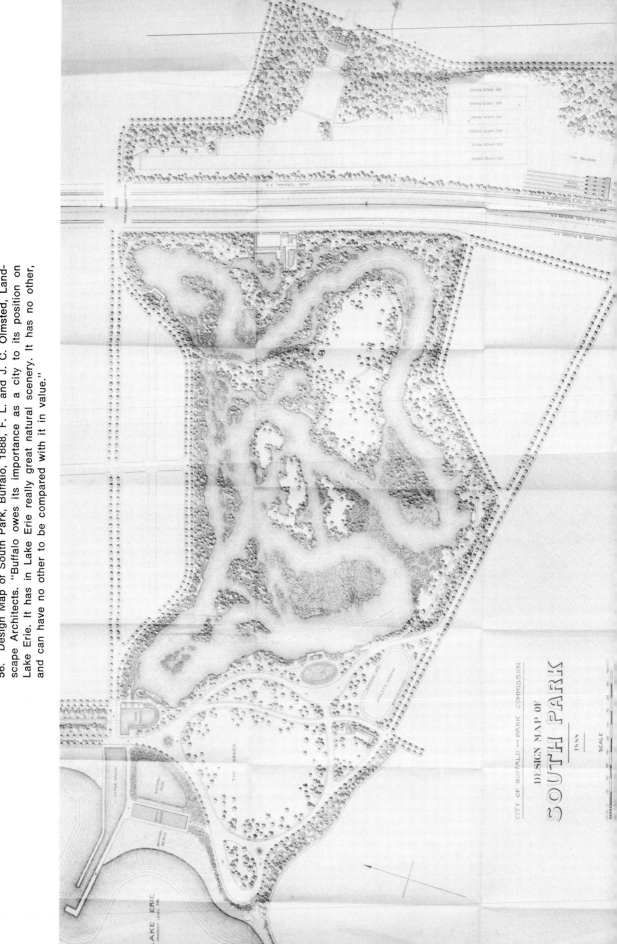

56. Design Map of South Park, Buffalo, 1888, F. L. and J. C. Olmsted, Landscape Architects. "Buffalo owes its importance as a city to its position on Lake Erie. It has in Lake Erie really great natural scenery. It has no other, and can have no other to be compared with it in value."

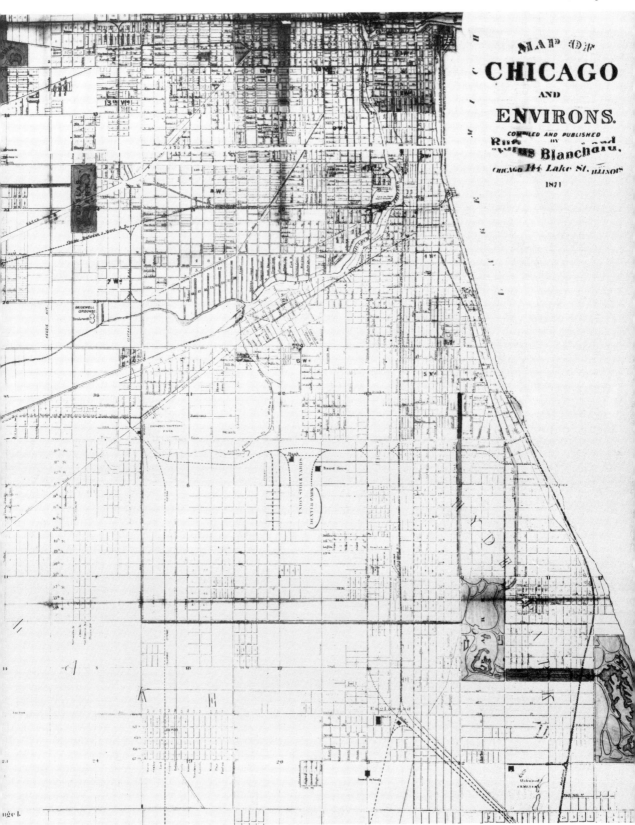

57. Map of Chicago and Environs, 1871, Rufus Blanchard. The flatness of the terrain and the general climatic conditions of Chicago made that city, in Olmsted's view, particularly "unfavourable to parks." To achieve and maintain a good park system would require, because of environmental conditions, a corps of men well trained in the scientific, aesthetic, and administrative aspects of urban open spaces. Courtesy of Chicago Historical Society.

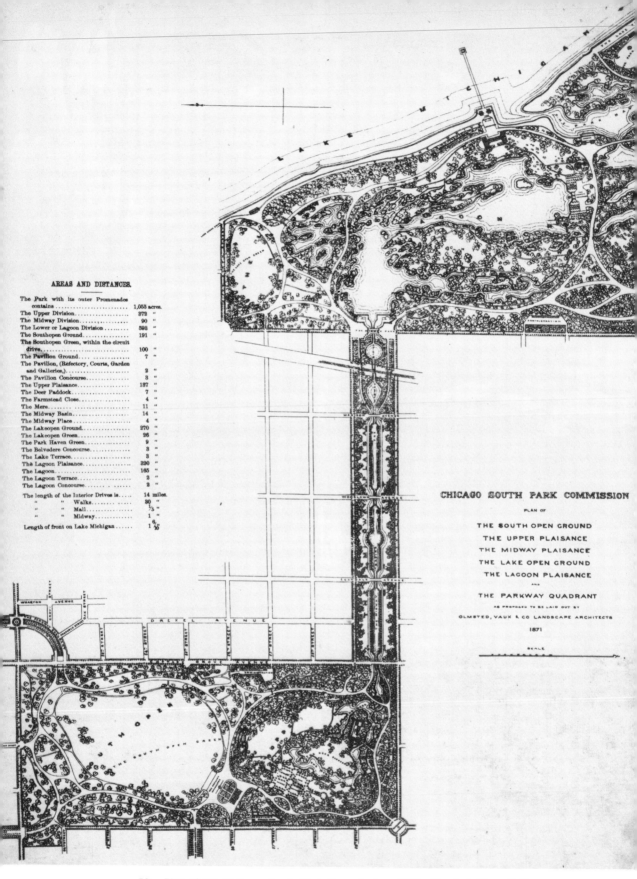

CHICAGO SOUTH PARK COMMISSION

PLAN OF

THE SOUTH OPEN GROUND
THE UPPER PLAISANCE
THE MIDWAY PLAISANCE
THE LAKE OPEN GROUND
THE LAGOON PLAISANCE
AND
THE PARKWAY QUADRANT

AS PROPOSED TO BE LAID OUT BY

OLMSTED, VAUX & CO LANDSCAPE ARCHITECTS

1871

SCALE

58. Plan of the Chicago South Park Commission, 1871, Olmsted, Vaux & Co.
The lower portion of South Park is now called Washington Park. The upper
park, Jackson Park, was to serve as a site for the World's Columbian Exposition (Fig. 59). "There is but one object of scenery near Chicago of special
grandeur or sublimity . . . the Lake."

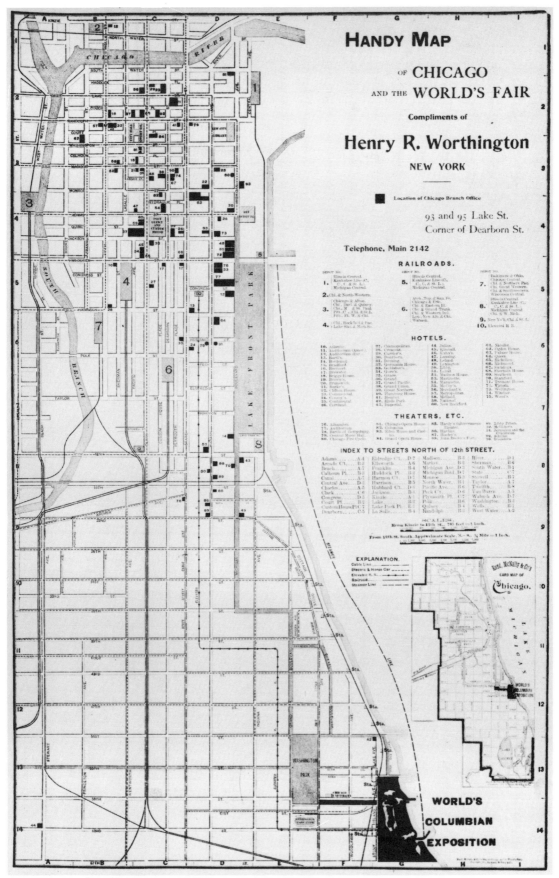

59. Handy Map of Chicago and the World's Fair, 1893. Of seven possible locations for the Fair, Olmsted proposed "the Jackson Park site [which] had, twenty years before, been selected as a site to be reserved for a public park" (See Fig. 3). Courtesy of Chicago Historical Society. (Olmsted's extended description of this plan appears, slightly edited, on p. 152, item 59.)

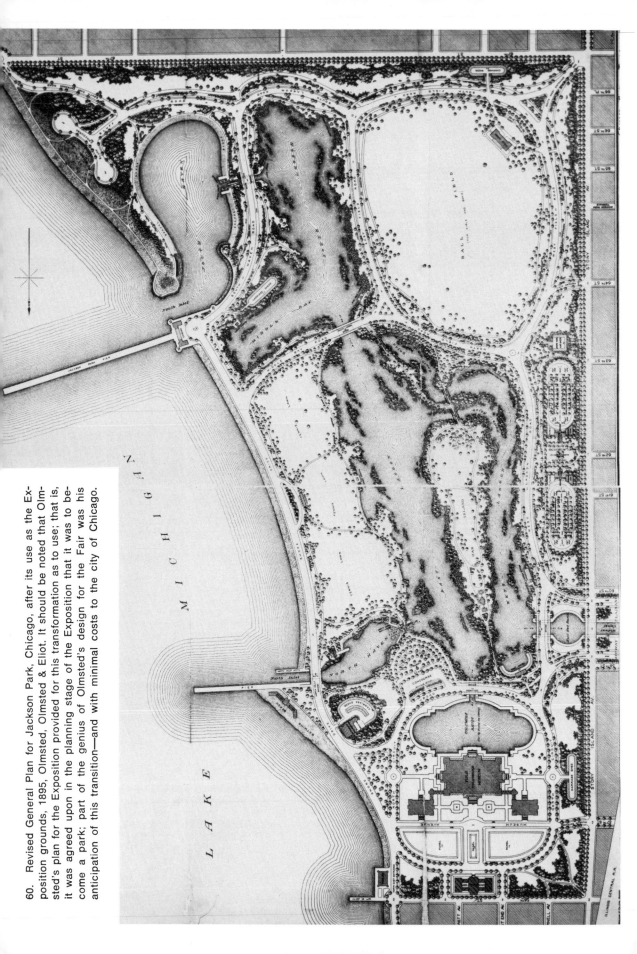

60. Revised General Plan for Jackson Park, Chicago, after its use as the Exposition grounds, 1895, Olmsted, Olmsted & Eliot. It should be noted that Olmsted's plan for the Exposition provided for this transformation as to use; that is, it was agreed upon in the planning stage of the Exposition that it was to become a park; part of the genius of Olmsted's design for the Fair was his anticipation of this transition—and with minimal costs to the city of Chicago.

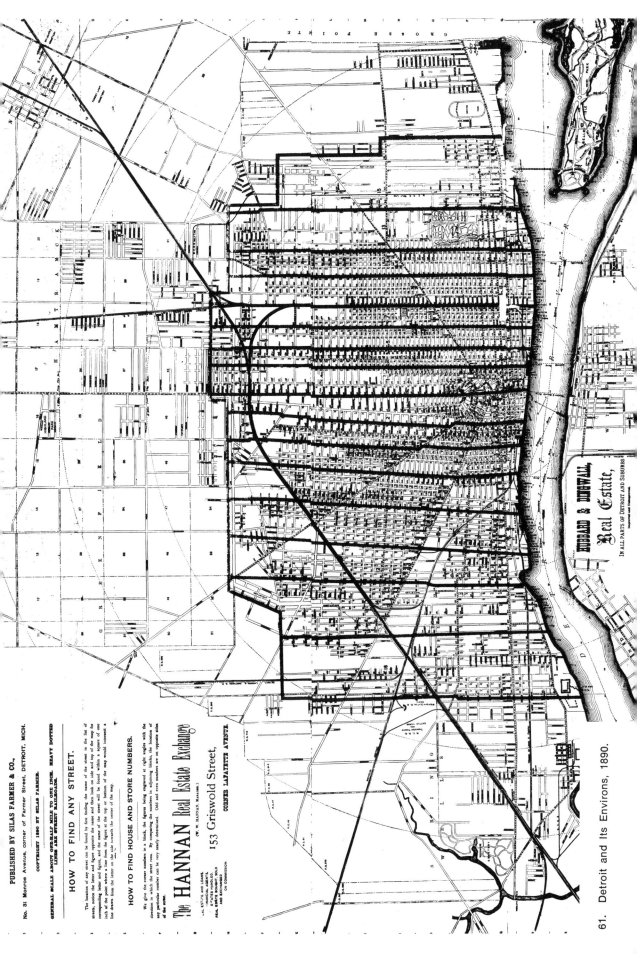

61. Detroit and Its Environs, 1890.

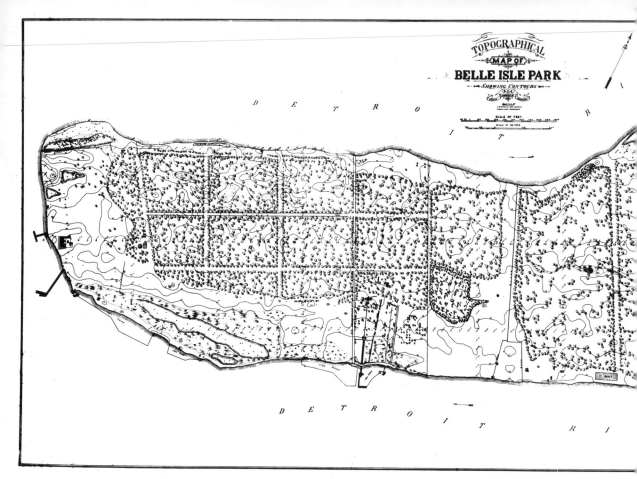

62. Topographical Map of Belle Isle Park, Detroit, ca. 1882. "The average elevation of [Belle Isle's] surface above that of the surrounding navigable waters is little more than two feet. Large parts are covered with well-grown wood, with much close underwood, beneath which . . . after every summer shower, there are puddles that gradually disappear more through evaporation than filtration. Other large parts are marshy; and in these there are constant pools, with rushy and bushy borders." A scientific understanding of the land —that is, of the total natural setting—is *basic* to the efforts of an environmental planner. A challenge to the planner-designer is that of fitting the social uses to the site, interfering with nature as little as possible. For the use of the site, see caption to Fig. 63.

63. Belle Isle Park, Detroit, Preliminary Plan, March 1883, F. L. Olmsted, Landscape Architect. "But Belle Isle must be regarded as combining, with the attractions of an ordinary urban park, not a little [of] those [attractions] of such suburban water-side resorts as are approached by steam-ferries from Portland, Portsmouth, Boston, Providence, New London, New York, Newark, Baltimore, and other coast-towns. It cannot fail to be greatly used in this way if properly prepared."

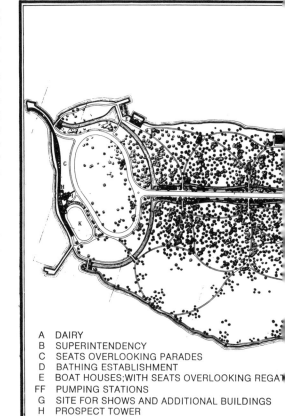

A DAIRY
B SUPERINTENDENCY
C SEATS OVERLOOKING PARADES
D BATHING ESTABLISHMENT
E BOAT HOUSES;WITH SEATS OVERLOOKING REGAT
FF PUMPING STATIONS
G SITE FOR SHOWS AND ADDITIONAL BUILDINGS
H PROSPECT TOWER
I REFECTORY
J SEATS OVERLOOKING GAMES
K MATCH GROUND

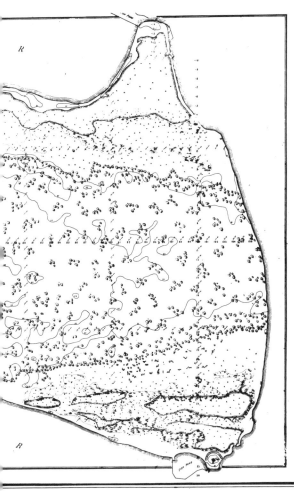

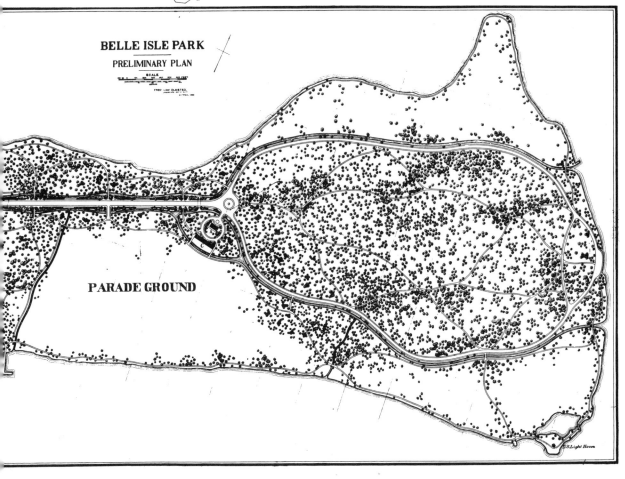

BELLE ISLE PARK

PRELIMINARY PLAN

SCALE

FRED· LAW OLMSTED,

PARADE GROUND

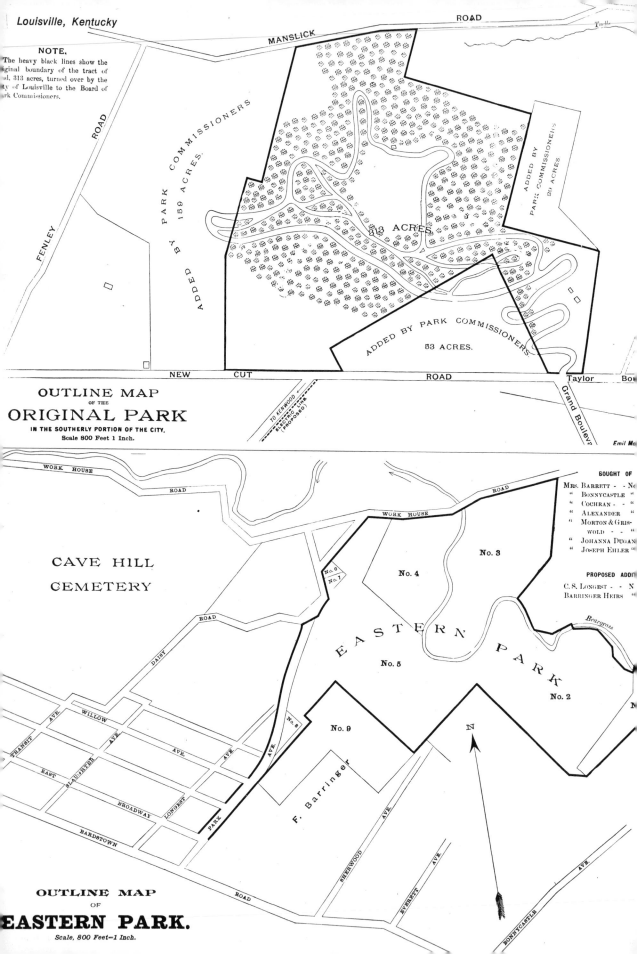

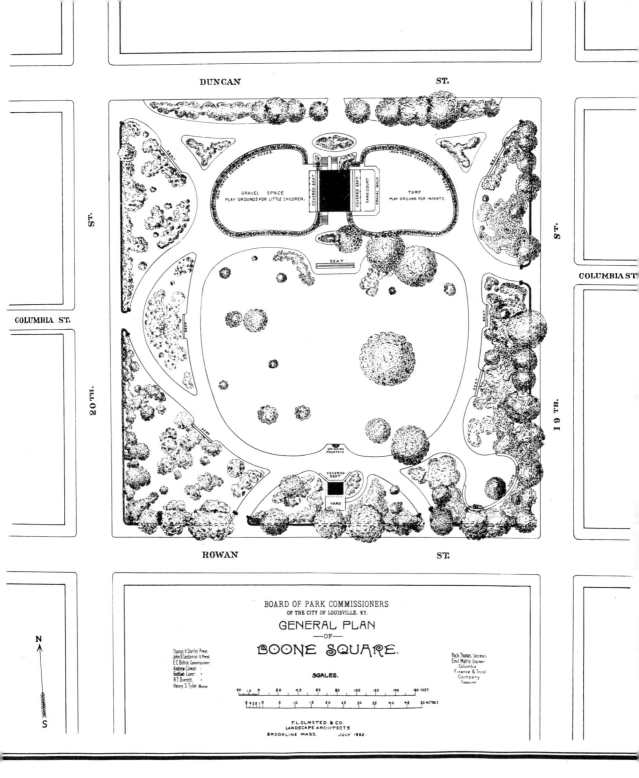

64. Outline Map of the Original [Iroquois] Park, ca. 1890, Emil Mahlo, Engineer. Olmsted urged the Park Commissioners of Louisville to maintain the natural topography of the site.

65. Outline Map of Eastern [Cherokee] Park, Louisville, ca. 1890.

66. General Plan of Boone Square, Louisville, July 1892, F. L. Olmsted & Co., Landscape Architects. "Boone Square is . . . a popular playground park in a densely settled district."

67. Boone Square, Louisville, a playground, 1892.

BOARD OF PARK COMMISSIONERS OF THE CITY OF LOUISVILLE, KY.

PLAN OF

KENTON PLACE

1892

SCALES

EMIL MAHLO
PARK ENGINEER

F. L. OLMSTED & CO.
LANDSCAPE ARCHITECTS.

MARKET

STREE

SHELBY

CAMPBELL

68. Plan of Kenton Place, Louisville, 1892, F. L. Olmsted & Co., Landscape Architects; Emil Mahlo, Park Engineer.

69. View of Montreal, 1829. "You have chosen to take a mountain for your park. . . . Small as your mountain is, it presents in different parts no little variety of mountain form and feature."

70. Plan of Mount Royal, Montreal, 1877, Frederick Law Olmsted. "I have designated eight topographical divisions of the mountain, each possessing natural characteristics distinguishing it from those adjoining." Olmsted gave to these divisions the names noted on the map.

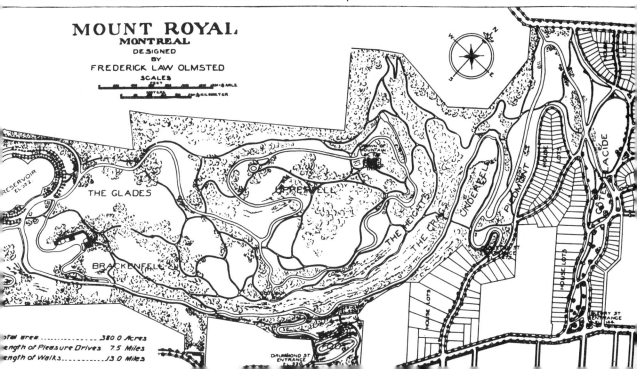

71. "Different Winding Roads of Crags' Foot,"
Mount Royal Park.

72. "Just out of Crags' Foot. The roads of Mount
Royal seem to fit a course."

Newport, Rhode Island

73. Map for Laying Out the Property of the Newport Land Trust at Newport,
1887, F. L. and J. C. Olmsted, Landscape Architects. "Whatever is to the
disadvantage of the air or the natural scenery of Newport . . . is disadvan-
tageous to the prosperity of the city."

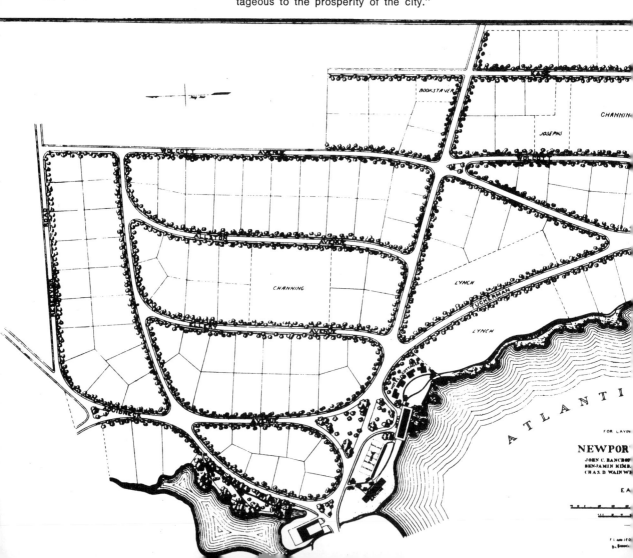

74. New York und Umgegend, 1867, Engraved by R. Kupfer, New York, Lithograph. Olmsted's experience in New York City shaped his career; he viewed New York as a "capital" city, where America's social and economic forces were concentrated, and where the future of planning would be determined; hence, failure or success of planning in New York was critical for the nation. He believed that if New York City adopted comprehensive land-use planning and management, the nation would follow suit—in the way that Central Park had touched off a nationwide urban park movement.

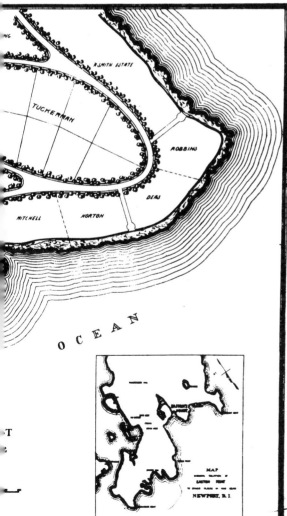

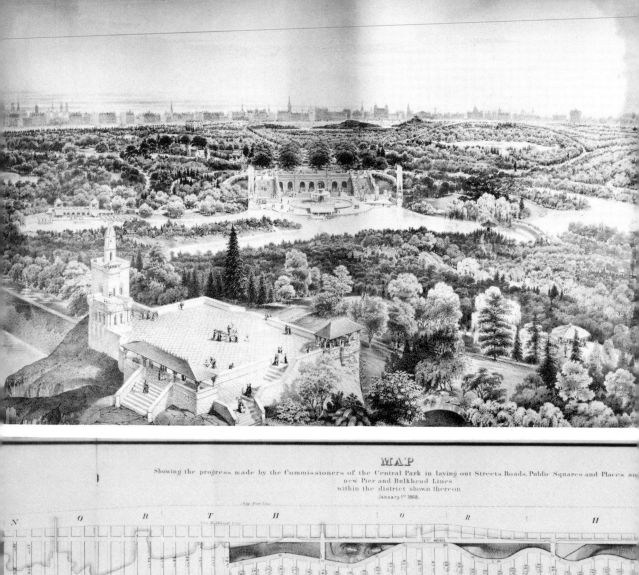

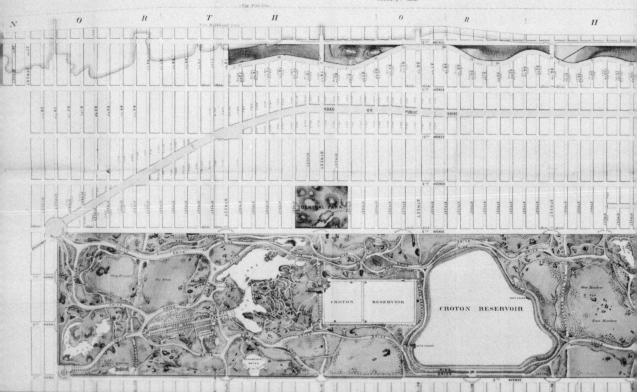

MAP
Showing the progress made by the Commissioners of the Central Park in laying out Streets, Roads, Public Squares and Places and new Pier and Bulkhead Lines
within the district shown thereon.
January 1st 1868.

N   O   R   T   H   O   R   T   H

ROAD   OR   PUBLIC   DRIVE

GENERAL PARK

CROTON   RESERVOIR

CROTON RESERVOIR

75. View of Central Park, ca. 1875. "[Central Park] was designed as a park to be situated at the precise centre of population of [a] city of two millions." The fact that the park was planned in anticipation of future open-space needs is but one reason why Central Park deserves to be considered the beginning of modern city planning. Its system of roads, separated interior spaces, and multiple recreational uses make it a model of planning for urban needs (See Figs. 87–94, 98–101).

76. Map Showing the Progress Made by the Commissioners of the Central Park in Laying Out Streets, Roads, Public Squares, and Places, and New Pier and Bulkhead Lines, 1868.

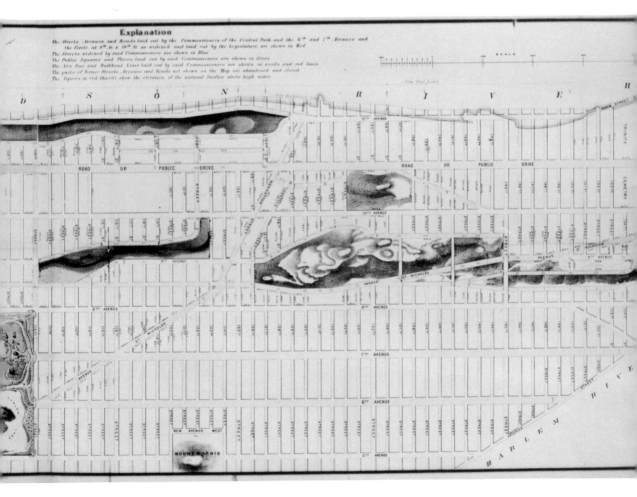

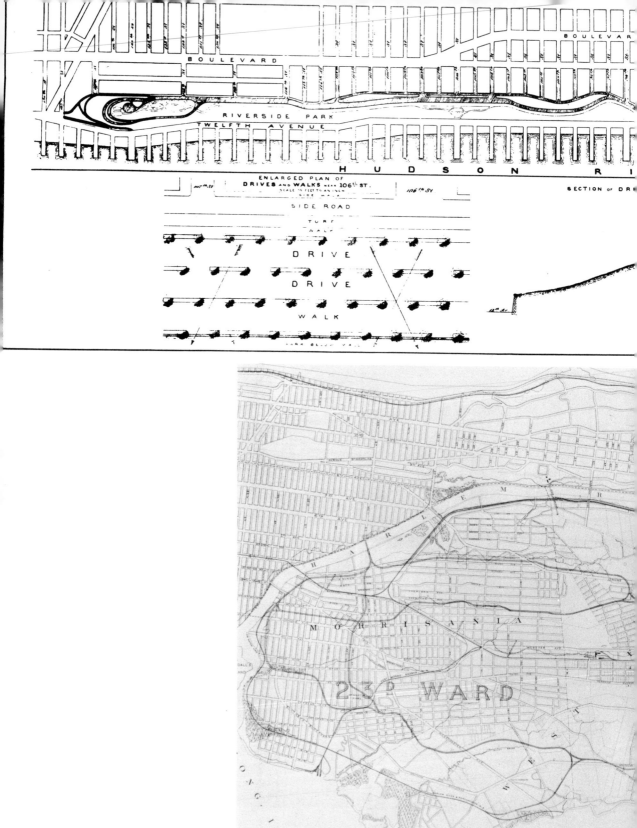

ENLARGED PLAN OF
DRIVES AND **WALKS** NEAR **106**TH ST.
SCALE 16 FEET TO AN INCH

BOULEVARD

RIVERSIDE PARK

TWELFTH AVENUE

H U D S O N   R I

SIDE ROAD

TURF

D R I V E

D R I V E

W A L K

SECTION OF DRE

H A R L E M   R

M O R R I S A N I A

2 3 D   W A R D

W E S T

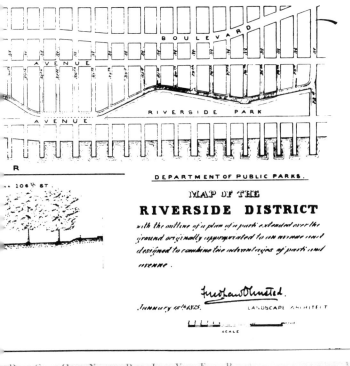

DEPARTMENT OF PUBLIC PARKS.

MAP OF THE
RIVERSIDE DISTRICT

with the outline of a plan of a park extended over the
ground originally appropriated to an avenue and
designed to combine the advantages of park and
avenue.

Fred Law Olmsted.

January 1st 1875.   LANDSCAPE ARCHITECT

SCALE

77. Map of the Riverside District, New York City, 1875, F. L. Olmsted.

78. Routes for Local Steam Transit in the Twenty-third and Twenty-fourth Wards of New York City, 1877, J. James R. Croes, Civil Engineer; F. L. Olmsted, Landscape Architect. This plan reflects the problem, basic to all planning, of whether a public agency—in this case, the Board of the Department of Public Parks—should determine a comprehensive transportation, road, and land-use plan prior to private development. Private interests won out over planning for the public good. (See note 96 to the text.)

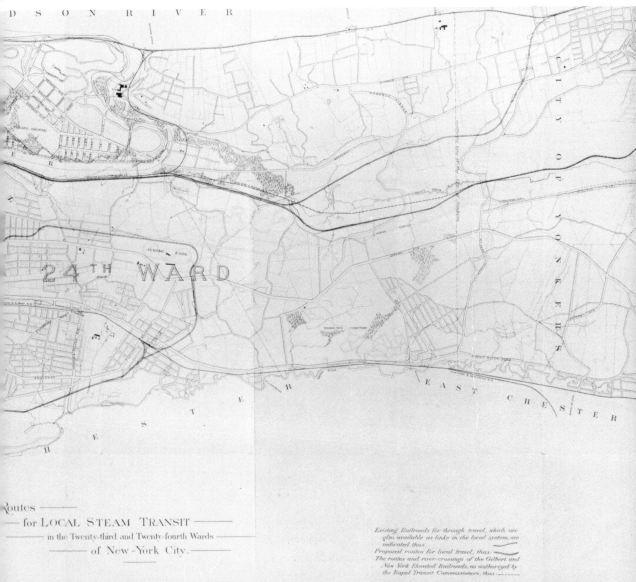

Routes
for LOCAL STEAM TRANSIT
in the Twenty-third and Twenty-fourth Wards
of New-York City.

SCALE

Existing Railroads for through travel, which are
also available as links in the local system, are
indicated thus
Proposed routes for local travel, thus
The routes and river-crossings of the Gilbert and
New York Elevated Railroads, as authorized by
the Rapid Transit Commissioners, thus

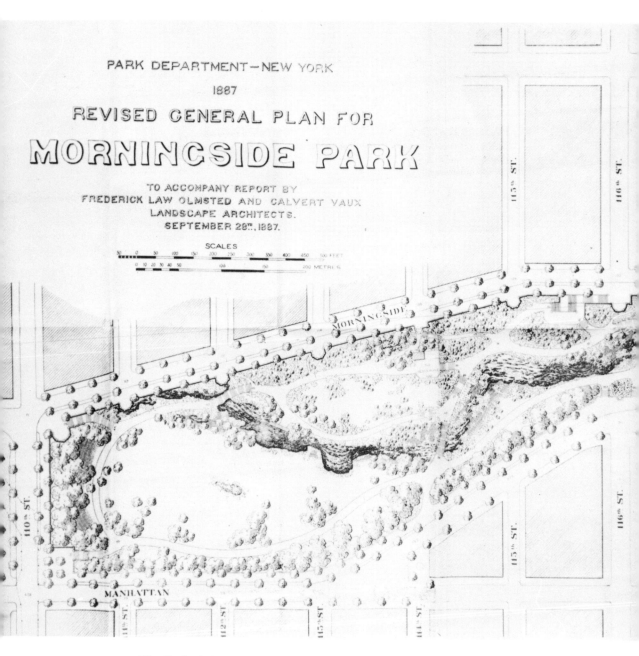

79. Revised General Plan for Morningside Park, New York City, 1887, F. L. Olmsted and C. Vaux, Landscape Architects.

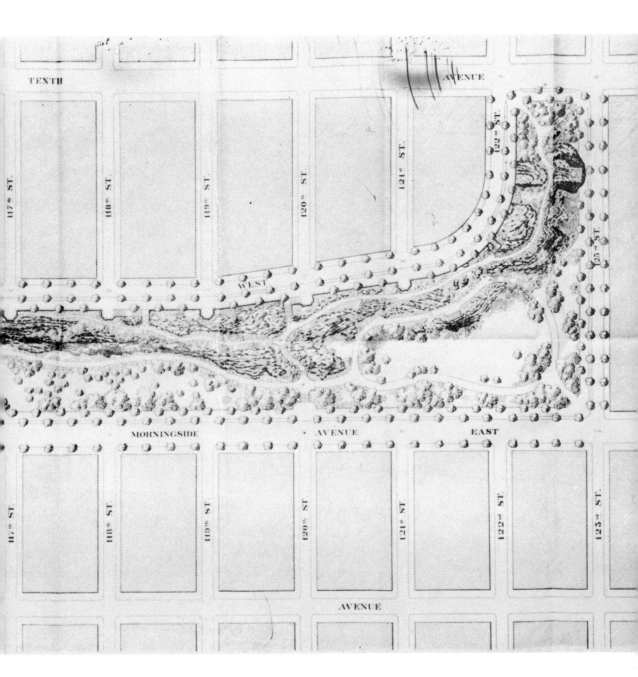

TENTH

117ᵗʰ ST.

118ᵗʰ ST.

119ᵗʰ ST.

120ᵗʰ ST.

121ˢᵗ ST.

122ᵈ ST.

AVENUE

123ᵈ ST.

WEST

MORNINGSIDE · AVENUE · EAST

117ᵗʰ ST.

118ᵗʰ ST.

119ᵗʰ ST.

120ᵗʰ ST.

121ˢᵗ ST.

122ᵈ ST.

123ᵈ ST.

AVENUE

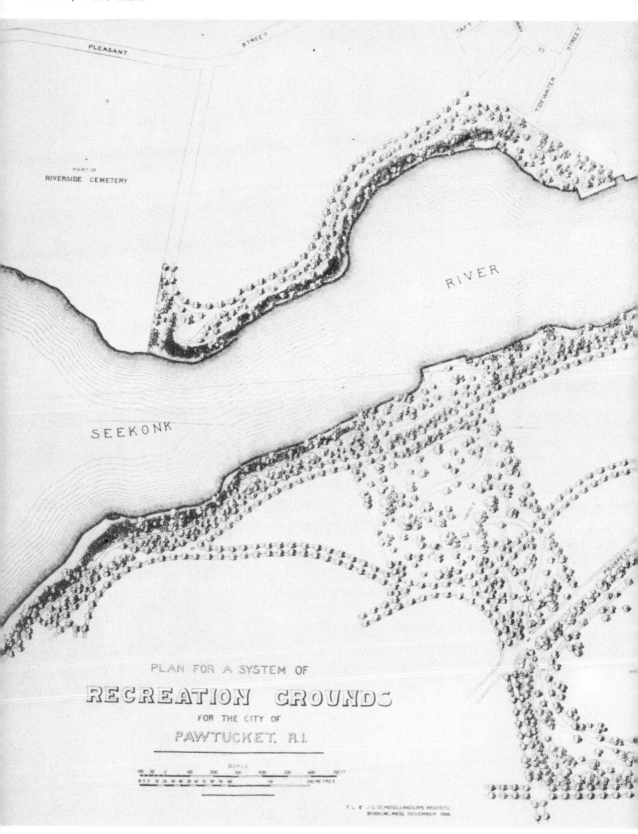

80. Plan for a System of Recreation Grounds for the City of Pawtucket, 1888, F. L. and J. C. Olmsted, Landscape Architects. "It may be laid down as a rule, that a city situated upon navigable water should see to it, if possible, that its people are provided with good arrangements for making recreative use of some portion of this water."

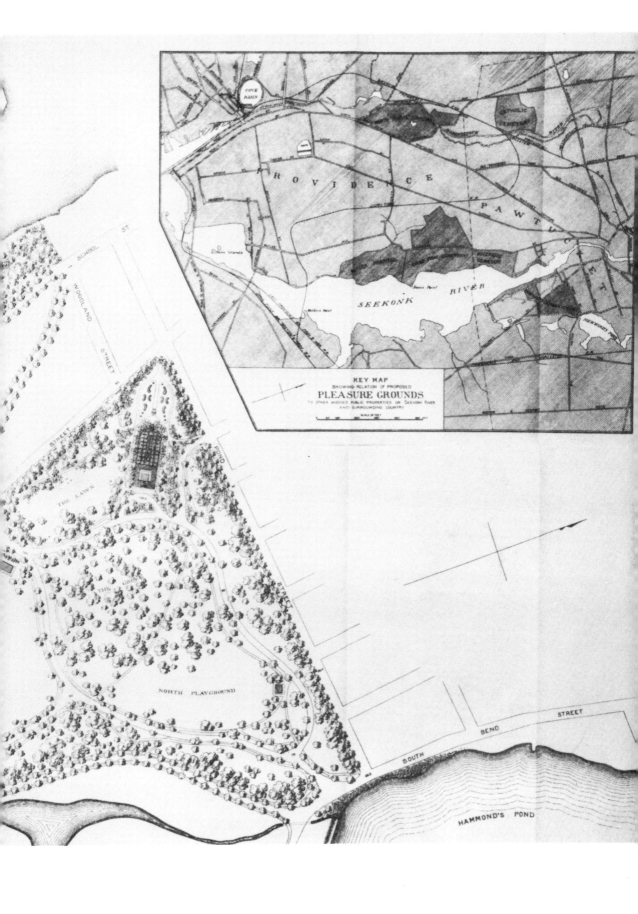

KEY MAP
SHOWING RELATION OF PROPOSED
PLEASURE GROUNDS
TO OTHER WOODED PUBLIC PROPERTIES ON SEEKONK RIVER
AND SURROUNDING COUNTRY

SCALE OF FEET

81.   Rochester, New York, 1890, Showing Genesee River Gorge and Seneca
Park (at top).

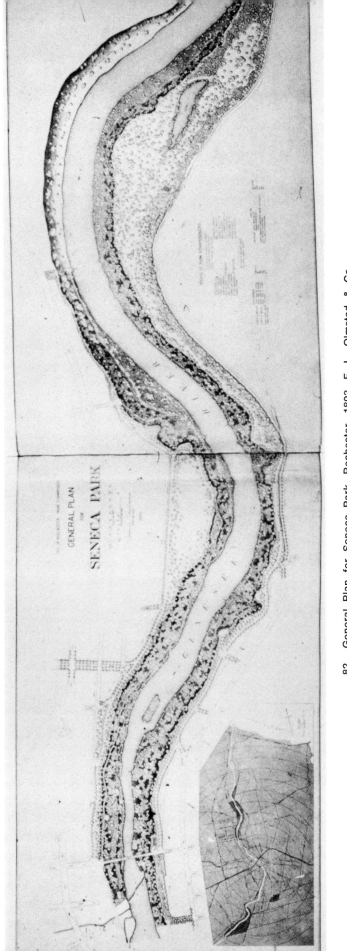

82. General Plan for Seneca Park, Rochester, 1893, F. L. Olmsted & Co., Landscape Architects.

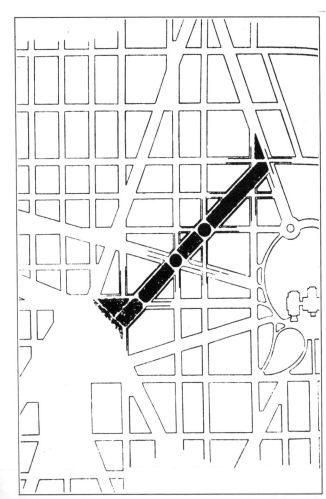

83. View of Washington, D.C., 1851, The Mall and Pennsylvania Avenue seen from Capitol Hill.

84. Map Showing Proposed Belt of Woods Between Public Grounds south of the Capitol Grounds, May 25, 1874, F. L. Olmsted, Landscape Architect. Washington, D.C., was considered unhealthy—particularly in summer. "If, therefore," Olmsted wrote, "there was a body of trees along the base of Capitol Hill, the ground beneath them being well drained and not in itself adapted to the production of malaria, it would in all probability be an efficient means of protection to the Capitol from malarial poison originating on the banks of the Potomac and in the low grounds between the river and the hill."

85. Washington, D.C., Capitol Approaches (west side) from F. L. Olmsted perspective drawing.

86. Washington, D.C., Drawing of the Capitol and its Grounds, by F. L. Olmsted, who did the landscaping. "The full proportions and beauty of a great building like the Capitol can only be comprehended from a distance at which its various parts will fall into a satisfactory perspective."

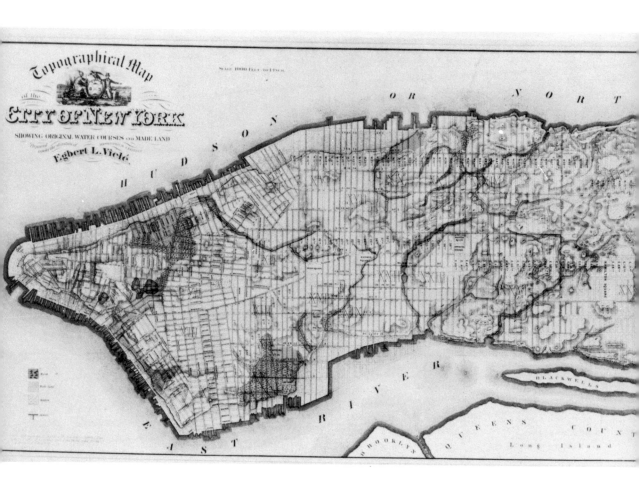

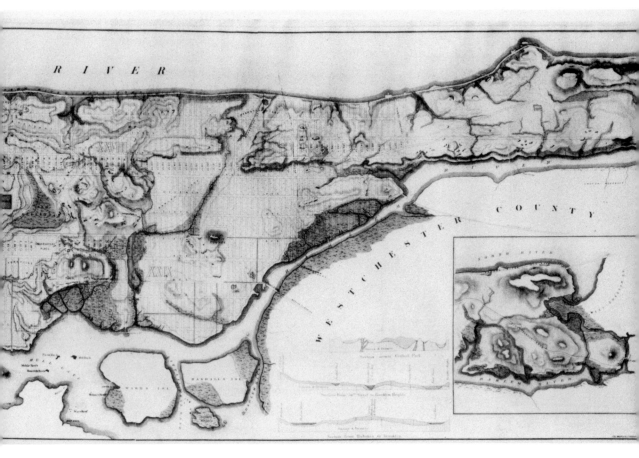

87. Topographical Map, City of New York. Showing Original Water Courses and Made Land, ca. 1859, Egbert L. Viele. Viele (1825–1902) was a prominent civil engineer who competed with Olmsted and Vaux to design both Central and Prospect parks. Although his designs were rejected, his topographical analysis of Manhattan Island remained an important source for all professionals interested in manipulating the surface and subsurface of the island (See Figs. 75, 76, 98–102).

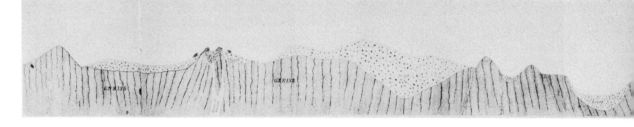

88. New York City. Section of Central Park from Fifth to Eighth Avenue, 1857.

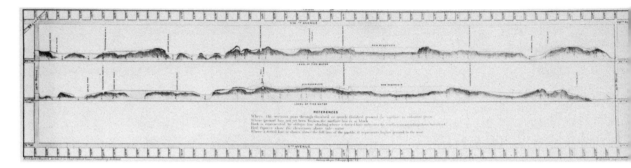

89. New York City. Profiles of Central Park on the lines of the Seventh and Eighth avenues prolonged from 59th to 100th streets, 1860.

90. Central Park: The Tunnel and Traffic Road, ca. 1860. "Preliminary to the construction of the Park roads a thorough survey of the grounds was necessary, and a careful location of the roads as to lines of direction, curves, grades, etc."

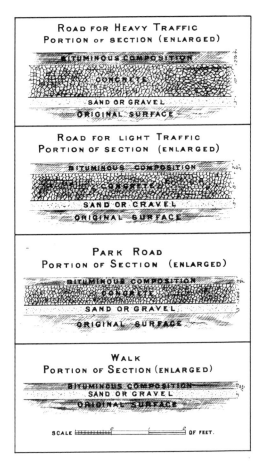

ROAD FOR HEAVY TRAFFIC
PORTION OF SECTION (ENLARGED)

BITUMINOUS COMPOSITION
CONCRETE
SAND OR GRAVEL
ORIGINAL SURFACE

ROAD FOR LIGHT TRAFFIC
PORTION OF SECTION (ENLARGED)

BITUMINOUS COMPOSITION
CONCRETE
SAND OR GRAVEL
ORIGINAL SURFACE

PARK ROAD
PORTION OF SECTION (ENLARGED)

BITUMINOUS COMPOSITION
CONCRETE
SAND OR GRAVEL
ORIGINAL SURFACE

WALK
PORTION OF SECTION (ENLARGED)

BITUMINOUS COMPOSITION
SAND OR GRAVEL
ORIGINAL SURFACE

SCALE ⊢⊢⊢⊢⊢⊢⊢⊢⊢ OF FEET.

91. Road Construction, Central Park, ca. 1865. "The scale upon which the Park roads have been constructed, and their general object, have been favorable for testing, in a thorough manner, some of the principal modes of road making . . . beyond ordinary practice in this country. . . ."

92. Central Park. Archway under carriage drive for traffic across the park, 1860.

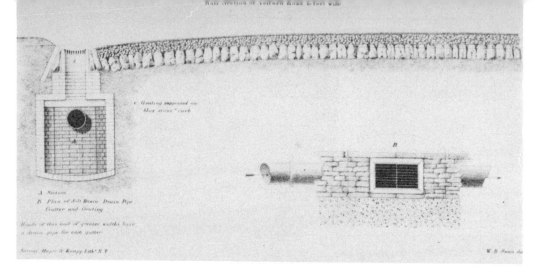

93. Central Park Carriage Roads, Drainage, 1862. "Without thorough drainage no superstructure, however well founded and otherwise skilfully built, will long resist the severe effects of our climate."

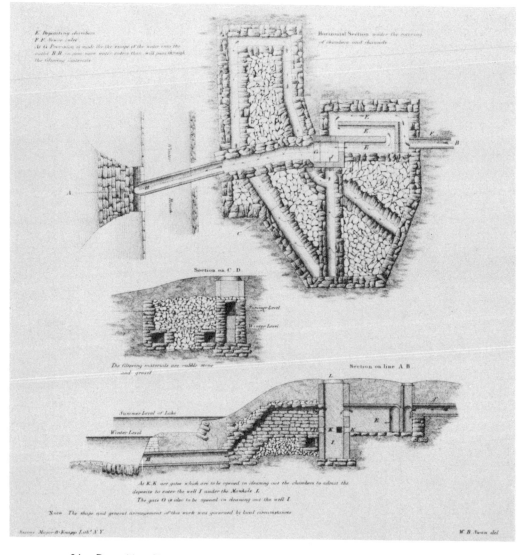

94. Depositing Chambers and Filter, Central Park, West Side of Lake. Sections.

95. Prospect Park, Tree Moving Machine, 1868.

96. Prospect Park, Brooklyn, Tree Trimming Machine, 1868.

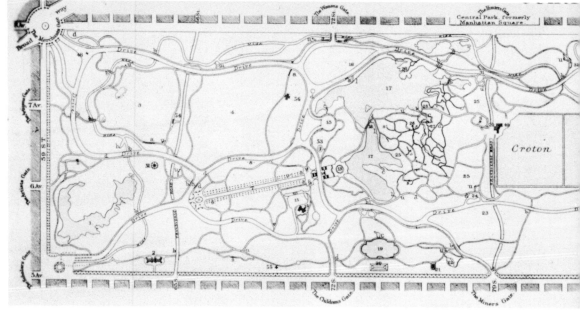

97.   Sheep Meadow, Franklin Park, Boston. "To sustain the designed character of the Country Park, the urban elegance generally desired in a small public or private pleasure ground is to be methodically guarded against. Turf, for example, is to be in most parts preferred as kept short by sheep, rather than by lawn mowers." (See Fig. 42.)

98.   Central Park Guide, ca. 1860. ". . . The drives, bridle-paths and walks [have been kept] entirely separate and distinct, so that visitors desiring to enjoy either recreation may do so without their pleasure being interfered with." (See Figs. 75, 76, 87–94.)

99.   Walking in Central Park. Archway Under Drive for Footpath Northeast of the Ramble, 1862.

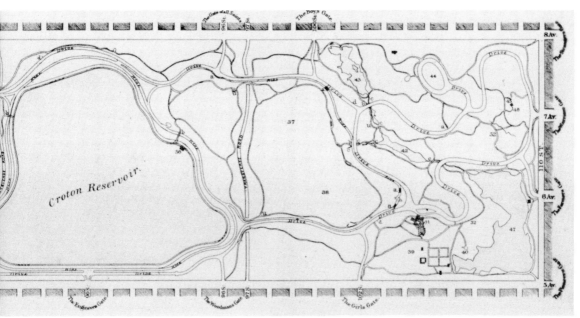

100. Horseback riding in Central Park. Archway Under Footpath for Bridle Road, South of the Meadows.

101. Walking, Riding, and Driving Simultaneously. Archway Under Drive for Bridle Road and Walk, Northwest of the Ramble in Central Park.

102. Music Pavilion to be erected on the Mall of Central Park. Engraving.

103. Mass Public Meetings. The Rostrum, Fort Greene, Brooklyn, to be erected ca. 1867.

104. Wading Pool in playground, ca. 1900, Delaware Park, Buffalo, New York (See Fig. 52).

105. Lawn Tennis, Franklin Park, Boston. "This ground is now for the most part boggy, and its surface strewn with boulders. The design is to convert it into a meadow adapted to be used (in the manner of the Long Meadow of the Brooklyn Park) for lawn games, such as tennis and croquet." (See Fig. 42.)

SOURCES OF QUOTATIONS
IN THE CAPTIONS

Complete references for the quotes from Olmsted are to be found in the list of Olmsted's writings (pp. 171–174).

Numbers refer to figure numbers.

2. Ralph Waldo Emerson, 1844. Quoted in Fein, ed., *Landscape into Cityscape,* p. 63.

3. Olmsted, "A Report . . . of the Columbian Exposition," *Architect and Building News,* p. 153.

4. Olmsted, Vaux & Co., *Report on Berkeley,* 1866, p. 25.

5. Olmsted, "Notes Explanatory of the Leading Motives of the Plan" (typewritten manuscript), 1886, Stanford University Archives.

8. Quoted in Hunt, p. 9.

17. Sylvester Baxter, *Boston Park Guide Including the Municipal and Metropolitan Systems of Greater Boston,* Boston, 1898, p. 35.

18. Baxter, *Boston Park Guide,* p. 29.

20. Quoted in Sylvester Baxter, *Lynn's Public Forest: A Hand-Book Guide to the Great Woods Park in the City of Lynn,* Boston, 1891, p. 25.

21. Olmsted, Vaux & Co., *Riverside,* p. 28.

23. Olmsted, Vaux & Co., *Columbia Institution for the Deaf and Dumb, Report,* p. 19.

24. Olmsted, *Mountain View Cemetery Report,* p. 48.

26. Olmsted et al., *Advisory Board Report on New Capitol,* p. 10.

28. Olmsted to [Warren] Manning, August 15, 1895, Manning Collection, Library, GSD, Harvard University.

30. Olmsted, "The Yosemite Valley . . . Preliminary Report," in *Landscape Architecture,* October 1952, p. 22.

31. Olmsted to William Dorsheimer, May 30, 1886, letterpress book, p. 365, Olmsted Papers.

32. Baxter, *Boston Park Guide,* p. 2.

37. Baxter, *Boston Park Guide,* p. 39.

39. Olmsted to Charles A. Dalton, December 29, 1881, Dec. 16, 1882, *Seventh Annual Report of the Board of Park Commissioners,* Boston, p. 26.

42. Olmsted to Dalton, op. cit., p. 26.

43. Baxter, *Boston Park Guide,* p. 37.

44. F. L. Olmsted and J. C. Olmsted, "Landscape Architects' Report," *Beardsley Park* (Boston, 1884), p. 6.

45. Olmsted, Vaux & Co., in *Landscape into Cityscape,* p. 99.

51. Olmsted, "Public Parks," *The Garden,* X (March 25, 1876), p. 299.

56. F. L. Olmsted and J. C. Olmsted, *The Projected Park . . . of Buffalo,* 1888, p. 8.

57. Olmsted, *The Garden,* X, p. 299.

58. Olmsted, Vaux & Co., *South Park Report,* 1871, p. 12.

59. Olmsted, "The Landscape Architecture of the World's Columbian Exposition," *The Inland Architect and News Record,* XXII (September 1893), p. 19.

THE DESIGN. The several elements of the scenery of Jackson Park are (1st) the Lake, (2nd) the Fields, and (3rd) the Lagoons.

The broad view of LAKE MICHIGAN will be commanded from a Shore Drive and from a Concourse on Sunrise Bluff. Steamboats may call at the long pier, where will be found the Casino restaurant. Sailboats may enter the park at the South Haven and steam launches and rowboats may enter and leave the North Haven by passing under North Inlet Bridge. Landings with floats will be found in both Havens for the use of boats coming from the Great Lake.

THE FIELDS lying between the Lagoons and the Lake and between the Lagoons and the South-west Entrance present broad and quiet landscape of the simplest pastoral sort which will be pleasingly commanded from the adjacent drives and walks. It is designed to allow strolling and the playing of tennis and croquet upon these fields. . . . Each field will have upon its border a building designed to supply to visitors shelter, light refreshments, and storage for wraps and the instruments of games.

THE LAGOONS, with their intricate and bushy shore lines, their beaches and bridges and their almost complete seclusion, offer scenery in striking contrast to that of the Lake Shore and Fields. . . . Landings for the use of electric omnibus boats and rowboats will be provided at convenient points and locks or runways will enable boats to be easily taken between the Lagoons and Havens . . . when the fluctuating water level of the Lake differs from the constant level which is necessary to preserve the marginal plant growths of the Lagoon.

Contrasting with the rest of the park, the neighborhood of the new building of the FIELD COLUMBIAN MUSEUM is designed upon formal lines for the sake of architectural harmony, as are the Music Court and a Gymnasium. . . . These formal parts of the park are intended to be lighted after dark and kept always open, but the more rural parks are designed to be closed at night.

62. *The Park for Detroit,* p. 22.

63. Olmsted, *Belle Isle: After One Year* (N.P., 1884), p. 13.

66. *Yearbook of the Board of Park Commissioners of Louisville, Kentucky* (1918), p. 54.

69. Olmsted, *Mount Royal,* p. 42.

70. *Mount Royal,* p. 43.

73. Olmsted, *Easton's Beach,* p. 10.

75. Olmsted to William Robinson, May 17, 1872, Olmsted Papers.

80. F. L. Olmsted and J. C. Olmsted, *Plan of . . . Pawtucket,* p. 11.

84. Olmsted to Edward Clark, May 23, 1874, U.S. Congress, 47th, 1st Session, Senate, Misc. Doc. No. 32, p. 2.

86. Olmsted to Edward Clark, October 1, 1881, in Edward Clark, Annual Report, 1881, p. 14.

90. W. H. Grant, "The New York 'Central Park,'" *The Franklin Institute Journal,* LIII (1865?), p. 297.

91. Grant, op. cit., p. 102.

93. Grant, op. cit., pp. 299–300.

97. Olmsted, *Franklin Park,* 1886, p. 53.

98. Clarence Cook, *Century Illustrated Monthly Magazine,* VI (September 1873), p. 533.

105. Olmsted, *Franklin Park,* p. 55.

NOTES

1. Thomas Carlyle and Ralph Waldo Emerson were important proponents of the theory that history is made by or reflected in the lives of "great men." Carlyle developed this theme in *Heroes and Hero Worship* (1841), in *Past and Present* (1843), and in *Oliver Cromwell's Letters and Speeches* (1845); a similar view was developed by Emerson in *Representative Men* (1850). Both Carlyle and Emerson were intellectual heroes to Olmsted.

2. For biographical details and an interpretation relating Olmsted's career to his times, see Charles E. Beveridge, "Frederick Law Olmsted: The Formative Years 1822–1865" (Ph.D. dissertation, University of Wisconsin, 1966); Albert Fein, "Frederick Law Olmsted: His Development As a Theorist and Designer of the American City" (Ph.D. dissertation, Columbia University, 1969); Albert Fein (ed.), *Landscape into Cityscape: Frederick Law Olmsted's Plans for a Greater New York City* (Ithaca, N. Y., 1968), Introduction; Charles McLaughlin, "Selected Letters of Frederick Law Olmsted" (Ph.D. dissertation, Harvard University, 1960).

Among the many aspects of Olmsted's biography that remain to be explained is the psychological basis of his need to undertake innovative challenging tasks even at the risk of his physical and mental well-being. There is a fairly clear pattern of a seeming willingness to accept punishment. One explanation of this pattern, I believe, is the fact that he lost his mother at the early age of four and was raised by a stepmother who, while dutiful and conscientious, was distant toward her adopted son and narrow in her commitment to fundamental Protestantism. At the same time, his father, who was the most kindly and considerate of parents, was also distant in his relationship with his son. In short, among the many factors that explain Olmsted's complex personality, talent, and achievements, one must consider these early relationships, which left an emotional void needing to be filled.

3. For an incisive analysis of the importance of environmental forms as national cultural goals, as reflected in the writings of America's leading authors, see Leo Marx, *The Machine in the Garden: Technology and the Pastoral Ideal in America* (New York, 1964).

4. For a perceptive literary analysis of this change as revealed in the cultural values of the period, see Larzer Ziff, *The American 1890s: Life and Times of a Lost Generation* (New York, 1966), Chapter 1. An excellent discussion of the ideological significance of the architecture of the Columbian Exposition is in Michael T. Klare's, "The Architecture of Imperial America," *Science and Society*, XXXIII (Summer–Fall), 257–84; I am indebted to Pro-

fessor George R. Collins for having brought this article to my attention. For an illuminating letter revealing Olmsted's awareness of this "stylistic" change and his own participation in it, see Olmsted to William Augustus Stiles, March 10, 1895, "Frederick Law Olmsted Papers" (Library of Congress), cited hereafter as Olmsted Papers.

5. Olmsted to Fred [?], August 10, 1886, Olmsted Papers. This evolution in planning theory can be traced by comparing the following three documents: "Frederick Law Olmsted and Calvert Vaux, Description of a Plan for the Improvement of the Central Park: 'Greensward' (1858 [1868 reprint])," in Fein (ed.), *Landscape into Cityscape,* pp. 63–88; Olmsted and Vaux, "Preliminary Report to the Commissioners for Laying Out a Park in Brooklyn, New York: Being a Consideration of Circumstances of Site and Other Conditions Affecting the Design of Public Pleasure Grounds (1866)," in *Landscape into Cityscape,* pp. 95–127; Olmsted, "Parks, Parkways and Pleasure-Grounds," *Engineering Magazine,* IX (May 1895), pp. 253–60.

6. Olmsted to Hon. W. F. Hayns [?], April 13, 1876; Salmon and De Stuckle to Olmsted, June 29, 1878; Olmsted to "Partners," July 24, 1892; Olmsted to John Charles Olmsted, August 6, 1892, Olmsted Papers.

7. For a fuller development of the park ideal, see Fein, "The American City: The Ideal and the Real," in *The Rise of an American Architecture,* ed. Edgar Kaufmann, Jr. (New York, 1970), pp. 51–112. For a discussion of Emerson's environmental concepts, see Marx, *Machine in the Garden,* pp. 227–54.

8. See, for example, Horace Bushnell, *Barbarism the First Danger* (New York, 1847).

9. For an excellent description of this reform spirit in Boston, see Arthur Mann, *Yankee Reformers in the Urban Age* (Cambridge, Mass., 1954).

10. Henry Van Brunt, *Richard Morris Hunt: A Memorial Address* (New York, 1896), pp. 14–15.

11. John V. Van Pelt, "Richard Morris Hunt," *Dictionary of American Biography,* ed. Dumas Malone (New York, 1932), IX, 390.

12. Olmsted to Richard Grant White, July 23, 1865, Richard Grant White Papers, New-York Historical Society—cited hereafter as White Papers. Olmsted was successful in persuading White as to the destructive effect that Hunt's design would have on the park's purpose: See Richard Grant White, "Gateways of the Central Park," *The Galaxy,* I (August 1866), pp. 650–56.

13. Richard M. Hunt, *Designs for the Gateways . . . the Southern Entrance of the Central Park* (New York, 1866), p. 6.

14. Olmsted to White, July 23, 1865, White Papers; Calvert Vaux to Clarence Cook, June 6, 1865, Olmsted Papers.

15. Vaux to Cook, June 6, 1865, Olmsted Papers.

16. Gifford Pinchot, *Breaking New Ground* (New York, 1947), p. 48.

17. Olmsted to Charles Eliot, April 29, 1895, Olmsted Papers.

18. Frederick L. Olmsted to Parke Godwin, August 1, 1858, Bryant-Godwin Papers, Manuscript Division, New York Public Library—cited hereafter as Bryant-Godwin Papers.

19. Olmsted to John Hull Olmsted, June 23, 1845, Olmsted Papers.

20. Olmsted to Calvert Vaux, November 26, 1863, Olmsted Papers.

21. Frederick L. Olmsted, *Walks and Talks of an American Farmer in England* (New York, 1852); Charles Loring Brace, *Hungary in 1851* (New York, 1852); and Brace, *Home-Life in Germany* (New York, 1856).

22. The best description of this aspect of Olmsted's career is in Laura Wood Roper's "Frederick Law Olmsted and the Western Texas Free-Soil Movement," *American Historical Review,* LVI (October 1950), 58–64; and idem, "Frederick Law Olmsted and the Port Royal Experiment," *Journal of Southern History,* XXXI (August 1965), pp. 272–84.

23. See Laura Wood Roper, "Frederick Law Olmsted in the 'Literary Republic,' " *Mississippi Valley Historical Review,* XXXIX (December 1952), 459–82; and " 'Mr. Law' and Putnam's Monthly Magazine: A Note on a Phase in the Career of Frederick Law Olmsted," *American Literature,* XXVI (March 1954), pp. 88–93.

24. See Charles J. Stillé, *History of the United States Sanitary Commission* (Philadelphia, 1866); see also William Q. Maxwell, *Lincoln's Fifth Wheel: The Political History of the United States Sanitary Commission* (New York, 1956), for an interpretation that stresses the political dynamics of the commission.

25. Frederick Law Olmsted, *Mariposa Estate: The Manager's General Report* (New York, 1864). For a more theoretical statement indicating the impact of Olmsted's California experience on his perspective, see "Mariposa—a Pioneer Community of the Present Day," manuscript, Olmsted Papers.

26. Parke Godwin, *A Popular View of the Doctrines of Charles Fourier* (2d ed.; New York, 1844), Chapter 1, pp. 7–18.

27. Henry W. Bellows, "Cities and Parks: With Special Reference to . . . Central Park," *Atlantic Monthly,* VII (April 1861), p. 416.

28. Olmsted, *Walks and Talks,* Part I, p. 2.

29. Brace, *Home-Life in Germany,* p. 251; Parke Godwin, "Future of the Republic," p. 51, ms., Bryant-Godwin Papers; Horace Bushnell, *The Principles of National Greatness* (New Haven, 1837), p. 14.

30. Olmsted, *Walks and Talks,* Part I, p. 225.

31. Frederick L. Olmsted, *Public Parks and the Enlargement of Towns* (Cambridge, Mass., 1870), pp. 1–2.

32. Frederick L. Olmsted, "The Beginning of Central Park: A Fragment of Autobiography (ca. 1877)," in Fein, ed., *Landscape into Cityscape,* p. 52.

33. Frederick L. Olmsted, autobiographical manuscript scrap, n.d., Olmsted Papers. As an example of the use of such statistical material, see Olmsted et al.: "Report to the Staten Island Improvement Commission of a Preliminary Scheme of Improvements (1871)," in Fein, ed., *Landscape into Cityscape,* pp. 284–300.

34. Frederick L. Olmsted and Calvert Vaux, "Report of the Landscape Architects and Superintendents to the President of the Board of Commissioners of Prospect Park, Brooklyn (1868)," in Fein, ed., *Landscape into Cityscape,* p. 149.

35. Frederick L. Olmsted et al.: "Report to the Staten Island Improvement Commission of a Preliminary Scheme of Improvements (1871)," ibid., p. 175.

36. Ibid.

37. Olmsted and Vaux, "Prospect Park . . . (1868)," ibid., pp. 149–50.

38. See Olmsted, "The Spoils of the Park," ibid., passim.

39. Olmsted to Charles L. Brace, January 11, 1851, Olmsted Papers.

40. Quoted in Frederick Law Olmsted, *A Journey in the Seaboard Slave States, with Remarks on Their Economy* (New York, 1856), pp. 297–98.

41. Frederick L. Olmsted, autobiographical manuscript scrap, n.d., Olmsted Papers.

42. Olmsted, *A Few Things to Be Thought of Before Proceeding to Plan Buildings for the National Agricultural Colleges* (New York, 1866), p. 10.

43. Olmsted, *Seaboard*, p. 425.

44. Frederick L. Olmsted to Charles E. Norton, April 26, 1866, Charles Eliot Norton Papers, Houghton Library, Harvard University—cited hereafter as Norton Papers.

45. Olmsted, Vaux & Co., *Preliminary Report in Regard to a Plan of Public Pleasure Grounds for the City of San Francisco* (New York, 1866), p. 15.

46. Olmsted, manuscript essay, "On Education," n.d., Olmsted Papers.

47. Olmsted, Vaux & Co., "Preliminary Report to the Commissioners for Laying Out a Park in Brooklyn, New York . . . (1866)," in Fein, ed., *Landscape into Cityscape*, p. 100.

48. John Eaton to Frederick L. Olmsted, October 24, 1882, Olmsted Papers. Eaton (1829–1906) served as U.S. Commissioner of Education from 1870 to 1886.

49. For further discussion of Olmsted's close working relationship with Richardson, see Mrs. Schuyler Van Rensselaer, *Henry Hobson Richardson and His Work* (New York, 1888), and Henry-Russell Hitchcock, *The Architecture of H. H. Richardson and His Times* (rev. ed.; Hamden, Conn., 1961).

50. For a good discussion of the relationship of social attitudes to disease in the first half of the nineteenth century, see Charles Rosenberg, *The Cholera Years* (Chicago, 1962). As Rosenberg notes (pp. 199–200), it was Koch who, in 1883, discovered in cholera vibrio the microscopic substance that "caused" the disease. It is interesting to note that the word "oecology" was first introduced into the English language in 1873—see *The Oxford English Dictionary*, Vol. II (Oxford, England, 1933), p. 64. We are all indebted to Dr. René Dubos for his many works, which have set into a historic context the relationship between ecology and health; see, for example, *Mirage of Health: Utopias, Progress and Biological Change* (New York, 1959).

51. For a discussion of Waring's early career, see James Cassidy, "The Flamboyant Colonel Waring," *Bulletin of the History of Medicine*, XXXVI (March–April 1962), 163–76; for Waring's later career, see Richard Skolnick, "George E. Waring Jr.: A Model for Reformers," *New-York Historical Society Quarterly*, LII (October 1968), 354–78. See William H. Grant, "The New York 'Central Park,'" *Journal of the Franklin Institute*, LIII (3d series, 1867), 233–38, 297–391, 394–97. For a brief biographical discussion of Pilat, see Katherine McNamara, "Ignaz Anton Pilat," *Dictionary of American Biography*, Vol. VII (New York, 1936), pp. 600–01.

52. The most comprehensive statement regarding the variety of park uses is to be found in the work of Olmsted's supporter Sylvester Baxter, *Boston Park Guide Including the Municipal and Metropolitan Systems of Greater Boston* (Boston, 1898). Baxter's work deals exclusively with the city of Boston and the surrounding region. For an example of Olmsted's plans for

multiuse individual parks, see Frederick Law Olmsted, *Mount Royal, Montreal* (New York, 1881). For an example of Olmsted's plan for an interrelated park system, see Olmsted, Vaux & Co., "Preliminary Report to the Commissioners for Laying Out a Park in Brooklyn, New York . . . 1866," in Fein, ed., *Landscape into Cityscape.* For an example of an urban park planned as a conservation area, see Frederick Law Olmsted & Co., "Report on Parks and Park-Making," in *First Annual Report of the Board of Park Commissioners of the City of Louisville* (Louisville, Ky., 1891), pp. 51–56. For a description of Olmsted's plan for the design and use of parkways, see Olmstead *[sic],* Vaux & Co., *Preliminary Report Respecting a Public Park in Buffalo* (Buffalo, 1869), pp. 25–27. For a description of Olmsted's thought regarding the need for smaller, more intensively used urban spaces for active recreation—such as playgrounds—see Frederick Law Olmsted, "Parks, Parkways and Pleasure-grounds," *Engineering Magazine,* IX (May 1895), p. 253.

53. Olmsted, Vaux & Co., Report of the Park Commissioners . . . for a Public Park for the City of Newark (Trenton, 1868), p. 13.

54. For a perceptive discussion of the origins of Llewellyn Park, see Christopher Tunnard, *The City of Man* (New York, 1953), pp. 183–87.

55. Olmsted et al., "Report to the Staten Island Improvement Commission," in Fein, ed., *Landscape into Cityscape,* p. 202.

56. Frederick Law Olmsted, *Public Parks and the Enlargement of Towns* (Cambridge, Mass., 1870), pp. 9–10.

57. Olmsted used Alexander Jackson Davis as a landscape and architectural consultant on the location and design of his house at Sachem's Head, Guilford, Connecticut. I am indebted to Mrs. Laura W. Roper for bringing this association to my attention. Olmsted to John Hull Olmsted, September 5, 1847; Olmsted to John Olmsted, October 27, 1847, letters in possession of Mrs. Roper.

58. For a brief history of Riverside, see Herbert J. Bassman, ed., *Riverside Then and Now* (Riverside, Ill., 1936).

59. For a good description of Riverside and its influence on the development of the garden city concept, see Walter L. Creese, *The Search for Environment* (New Haven, Conn., 1966), pp. 153–57.

60. Olmsted, Vaux & Co., *Preliminary Report Upon the Proposed Suburban Village at Riverside, Near Chicago* (New York, 1868), p. 10.

61. Ibid., p. 19.

62. Ibid., p. 17.

63. Ibid., pp. 27–29.

64. Andrew J. Downing et al., "Report of the Commissioners Appointed to Mature and Report a Plan for an Agricultural College and Experimental Farm," New York State Assembly Document No. 30, January 2, 1850. See also Dr. W. W. Hall, *Health of Farmers' Families,* in Report of the Commissioner of Agriculture, House of Representatives Ex. Doc. No. 78 (Washington, D.C., 1863).

65. Downing et al., "Report . . . for an Agricultural College," p. 13.

66. Ibid., pp. 11–14.

67. For an interpretative biographical sketch of Morrill, see T. D. Seymour Bassett, "Nature's Nobleman: Justin Morrill, a Victorian Politician," *Vermont History: The Proceedings of the Vermont Historical Society,* XXX (January

1962). For Morrill's support of Olmsted, see *Documentary History of the Construction and Development of the U.S. Capitol Building and Grounds,* U.S. Congress, 58th, 2d Session, 1904, pp. 1156–63.

68. George W. Atherton, *The Legislative Career of Justin S. Morrill,* address delivered at New Haven, Connecticut, November 14, 1900 (Harrisburg, Pa., 1900), p. 18.

69. Ibid., p. 19.

70. Olmsted, Vaux & Co., *Architect's Report to the Board of Trustees of the College of Agriculture and the Mechanic Arts, of the State of Maine,* 46th Legislature, House Document No. 57 (Maine, 1867), p. 21. This was the second document Olmsted produced on agricultural colleges. The first was a plan for the agricultural college at Amherst, Mass., which was republished as *A Few Things to Be Thought of Before Proceeding to Plan Buildings for the National Agricultural Colleges* (New York, 1866). The same point of view was expressed in both documents.

71. Olmsted, Vaux & Co., *Report to . . . State of Maine,* pp. 22, 28.

72. Ibid., pp. 22–23.

73. Frederick L. Olmsted, "The Yosemite Valley and the Mariposa Big Trees [1865]," with an introductory note by Laura Wood Roper, *Landscape Architecture,* XLIII (October 1952), passim.

74. "American War Letters," July 22, 1864; copies of this correspondence were given to the author by Mrs. Jessie Field of Warwick, England. The author of this letter was Harriet Errington, a sister-in-law of Alfred Field, who had married Charlotte Errington of Staten Island. The Fields were close friends of the Olmsteds.

75. Quoted in Paul Herman Buck, *The Evolution of the National Park System of the United States* (Washington, 1946), p. 33. Roper, *Landscape Architecture,* p. 12.

76. For a summary of some of the politics of park planning in Boston, see Geoffrey Blodgett's excellent work *The Gentle Reformers: Massachusetts Democrats in the Cleveland Era* (Cambridge, Mass., 1966), pp. 125–27.

77. Peter A. Porter, "Historic Niagara," *The Niagara Book* (New York, 1901), pp. 118–19; Ronald L. Way, *Ontario's Niagara Parks: A History* (Niagara Falls, 1946), pp. 15–17.

78. Frederick L. Olmsted, "Notes by Mr. Olmsted," *Special Report of New York State Survey on the Preservation of the Scenery of Niagara Falls and Fourth Annual Report on the Triangulation of the State for the Year 1879* (Albany, 1880), pp. 27–31.

79. John Foord, *The Life and Public Services of Andrew Haswell Green* (New York, 1913), pp. 218–19.

80. Ibid., p. 219

81. Olmsted to James T. Gardiner, October 3, 1879, James T. Gardiner Papers, New York State Library, Albany, New York—cited hereafter as Gardiner Papers.

82. Foord, *Andrew Haswell Green,* p. 220.

83. Olmsted to Gardiner, October 1, 1879, Gardiner Papers.

84. J[onathan] B. Harrison, "Studies in the South," *Atlantic Monthly,* XLIV–L (1882–83). Norton to Olmsted, March 4, 1882, Olmsted Papers.

85. J[onathan] B. Harrison, "A Plea for Preservation," in *Notes on Niagara* (Chicago, 1883), p. 156.

86. Foord, *Andrew Haswell Green,* p. 221.

87. Olmsted to Norton, March 14, 1883, Norton Papers.

88. Olmsted to William Dorsheimer, May 30, 1886, letterpress book, p. 365, Olmsted Papers.

89. Olmsted, "The Customs and Evils of Patronage Explained and Set Forth," manuscript draft, ca. 1875, Olmsted Papers. See Olmsted, "Spoils of the Park," in Fein, ed., *Landscape into Cityscape,* passim.

90. Olmsted, "The Beginning of Central Park: A Fragment of Autobiography (ca. 1879)," in Fein, ed., *Landscape into Cityscape,* p. 57.

91. For the immediate reaction to Darwinian thought, see Walter Harding, *The Days of Henry Thoreau* (New York, 1965), p. 429.

92. For a seminal discussion of social Darwinism, see Richard Hofstadter, *Social Darwinism in American Thought* (rev. ed.; Boston, 1955); see also Russel B. Nye, "Comment on C. Vann Woodward's Paper," in *New Frontiers of the American Reconstruction,* ed. Harold M. Hyman (Urbana, Ill.; 1966), pp. 148–56.

93. Olmsted, "Parks: A Glance Back and Forth," manuscript draft, n.d., Olmsted Papers.

94. *Putnam's Monthly Magazine,* VII (January 1856), 99: Olmsted to Mrs. Frederick L. Olmsted, March 2, 1863, Olmsted Papers.

95. Olmsted, "The Customs and Evils of Patronage Explained and Set Forth," Olmsted Papers.

96. The bitter clash of views between Olmsted and the Board can be discerned from two public documents. Olmsted's point of view is set forth in a report prepared by him and a civil engineer, J. James R. Croes, Document No. 72 of the Board of the Department of Public Parks: "I. Preliminary Report of the Landscape Architect and the Civil and Topographical Engineer, upon the Laying Out of the Twenty-third and Twenty-fourth Wards: II. Report Accompanying a Plan for Laying Out that Part of the Twenty-fourth Ward, Lying West of the Riverdale Road (1876)," in Fein, ed., *Landscape into Cityscape,* pp. 349–73. In this plan, Olmsted urged the comprehensive development of the territory as a "suburb" before the selling of property. It was an effort to plan the public facilities requisite to a model residential community prior to settlement; however, for members of the Board of Commissioners of Public Parks and others, the need for quick settlement of the area by traditional methods of land subdivision was paramount.

For the official viewpoint, see "Report of Commissioner Stebbins upon the Plans for Laying Out that Part of the Twenty-fourth Ward Lying West of Riverdale Road," *Board of the Department of Public Parks* (New York, February 28, 1877), Document No. 74, p. 12. Stebbins described Olmsted's proposal as "a hazardous experiment, which has no sanction either in practice or in the intentions of the law which has conferred upon the Board the responsibility of this important work."

97. Olmsted to Norton, December 14, 1884, Norton Papers.

98. Olmsted to Norton, March 16, 1886, Olmsted Papers.

99. J[onathan] B. Harrison, *Notes on Industrial Conditions* (Franklin Falls, N.H., 1886), p. 27.

100. See, for example, Olmsted's forward-looking article, "The Future of New York," *New York Daily Tribune* (December 28, 1879), p. 5, in which he sets out the importance of New York as a "capital" city.

101. For an interesting analysis of this use of plant materials, see Thorstein Veblen, "The Theory of the Leisure Class," in *The Portable Veblen,* ed. Max Lerner (New York, 1948), pp. 171–72. Veblen held that "the popular taste in these matters is to be seen in the prevalent high appreciation of topiary work and of the conventional flower-beds of public grounds." Commenting on Jackson Park, Chicago, after Olmsted had withdrawn from professional practice, Veblen wrote: "The artistic effects actually wrought in this work of reconstruction diverge somewhat widely from the effect to which the same ground would have lent itself in hands not guided by pecuniary canons of taste."

102. For a good biographical sketch of Ward, see Henry Steele Commager, ed., *Lester Ward and the Welfare State* (Indianapolis, 1967), Introduction.

103. Frederick L. Olmsted, ". . . Paper Relating to the Trees, Shrubs, and Plants in the United States Capitol Ground, and an Index of the Same Together with Some Observations upon the Planting and Care of Trees in the District of Columbia," in *Annual Report of the Architect [Edward Clark] of the United States Capitol for the Fiscal Year Ending June 30, 1882* (Washington: Government Printing Office, 1882), pp. 11, 13.

104. Frederick L. Olmsted and J[onathan] B. Harrison, *Observations on the Treatment of Public Plantations, More Especially Relating to the Use of the Axe* (Boston, 1889), p. 14. See F. L. Olmsted and Co., "Report on Parks and Park-Making," in *First Annual Report of the Board of Parks Commissioners of the City of Louisville* (Louisville, Ky., 1891).

105. Olmsted to John Charles Olmsted, April 10, 1886; Olmsted to Charles E. Norton, March 16, 1886, Olmsted Papers.

106. Olmsted to J. G. Aster, October 29, 1888; Olmsted to Mr. Gall, October 30, 1888; Olmsted to Mr. Douglass, April 18, 1889; Olmsted to "Partners," November 8, 1893, and May 3, 1894, Olmsted Papers.

107. Olmsted to "Partners," June 18, 1893; May 3, 1894—Olmsted Papers; Olmsted to Mr. Gall, July 7, 1894, Olmsted Papers.

108. Olmsted to Charles Eliot, April 29, 1895; Olmsted to "Partners," April 3, 1895; Olmsted to Charles Eliot, April 29, 1895, Olmsted Papers.

109. Carl Alwin Schenck, *The Biltmore Story: Recollections of the Beginning of Forestry in the United States,* ed. by Ovid Butler (St. Paul, Minn., 1955), passim.

110. William Dean Howells, Introduction to Edward Bellamy, *The Blindman's World and Other Stories* (New York, 1968 [from an 1898 ed.]), p. 1.

111. For an evaluation of Bellamy's thought, see Robert L. Shurter, "The Writing of *Looking Backward,*" *South Atlantic Quarterly,* XXXVIII (July 1939), p. 258; Robert H. Bremner, *From the Depths: The Discovery of Poverty in the United States* (New York, 1956), p. 25; and Edward Bellamy, *Looking Backward 2000–1887* (Houghton Mifflin, Boston, 1926), Introduction by Sylvester Baxter, p. 56.

112. Shurter, "The Writing of *Looking Backward*," pp. 257, 259–60; Mann, *Yankee Reformers,* p. 15.

113. Bellamy, *Looking Backward,* p. 323.

114. Ibid., p. 38.

115. Ibid., p. 243.

116. For Baxter's appreciation of Bellamy, see his Introduction to *Looking Backward;* for a brief biographical sketch of Baxter, see George R. Collins and Christiane Crasemann Collins, *Camillo Sitte and the Birth of Modern City Planning* (New York, 1965), p. 138. Olmsted to Baxter, March 24, 1886, Olmsted Papers.

117. Sylvester Baxter, "The Boston Metropolitan Park Movement," *Garden and Forest,* V (February 10, 1892), p. 62. For a description of the Boston Regional Park System, see Andrew W. Crawford, *The Development of Park Systems in American Cities (Philadelphia, 1905),* pp. 21–23. For political aspects of the commission, see Blodgett, *The Gentle Reformers,* p. 126.

118. For biographical details, see George T. Clark, *Leland Stanford War Governor of California, Railroad Builder and Founder of Stanford University* (Stanford University, 1931); Oscar Lewis, *The Big Four: The Story of Huntington, Stanford, Hopkins, and Crocker, and of the Building of the Central Pacific* (New York, 1938); Matthew Josephson, *The Robber Barons* (New York, 1962), pp. 81–89. Olmsted to George L. Waring, Jr., March 14, 1887 (letterpress book), p. 672, Olmsted Papers; see also Thomas H. Douglas to Olmsted, June 10, 1889, University Archives, Stanford University. Olmsted to Charles W. Eliot, June 8, 1886, Olmsted Papers.

119. Olmsted to Charles W. Eliot, June 10, 1886; Olmsted to Charles Eliot, July 20, 1886; Henry Sargent Codman to Olmsted, February 17, 1889; Olmsted to Frederick Law Olmsted, Jr., August 1, 1894[?], Olmsted Papers.

120. Henry Sargent Codman to Thomas H. Douglas, January 17, 1890, University Archives, Stanford University. W. R. Dudley, "Olmsted's Original Plans of Stanford University Grounds," *The Stanford Alumnus* (December 1906), pp. 129–35.

121. Olmsted to Mariana Griswold Van Rensselaer, April 9, 1888, Olmsted Papers.

122. Charles S. Sargent, "Park Boards and Their Professional Advisers," *Garden and Forest,* VII (November 21, 1894), p. 461. For a recent study of Sargent's contribution to the planning of the Arnold Arboretum and his association with Olmsted, see S. B. Sutton, *Charles Sprague Sargent and the Arnold Arboretum* (Cambridge, Mass., 1970), pp. 53–73.

123. Schenck, *The Biltmore Story,* p. 37.

124. Thomas F. Gilroy, Proclamation (n.p., 1893), Mayor's Papers, New York City Municipal Archives.

125. Quoted in Charles Moore, *Daniel H. Burnham, Architect Planner of Cities,* I (Boston, 1921), p. 79.

126. Charles Zueblin, *A Decade of Civic Improvement* (Chicago, 1905), pp. 60–61.

127. Olmsted, "A Report Upon the Landscape Architecture of the Columbian Exposition to the American Institute of Architects," *Architects and Building News,* XLI (September 9, 1892), p. 151.

128. For this meaning of the Fair, see Edgar Lee Masters, *The Tale of Chicago* (New York, 1933), pp. 194–262.

129. Olmsted to W. A. Stiles, October 7, 1892, Olmsted Papers.

130. Ibid. It is regrettable that Olmsted never completed the work on American history that he had begun, for it would have clarified the interfaces of his multifaceted contributions to American civilization.

131. The key figure in this renaissance is Lewis Mumford, whose *Brown Decades: A Study of the Arts in America, 1865–1895* (2d ed.; New York, 1955), first restored perspective on the contribution of Olmsted and his generation. It was Mumford's close friend, the great literary scholar Van Wyck Brooks, who, in *The Flowering of New England, 1815–1865* (New York, 1936), reconstructed the cultural context of the years in which Olmsted developed his principles of environmental planning.

BRIEF CHRONOLOGY OF THE LIFE OF FREDERICK LAW OLMSTED

1822	Born April 26 in Hartford, Connecticut, of Charlotte Law (Hull) and John Olmsted.
1826	Mother died.
1827	Father remarried (Mary Ann Bull).
1826–37	Primary education at various boarding schools in rural Connecticut.
1837–40	Served apprenticeship as a civil engineer.
1840–42	Employed as clerk for dry-goods importing firm, Benkard and Hutton, in New York City.
1843–44	Worked as cabin boy on the bark *Ronaldson* on trip to China.
1844–45	Served apprenticeships as farmer. Studied scientific agriculture at Yale University under Benjamin Silliman.
1846	Apprentice farmer to George Geddes, in Onondaga County, N. Y.
1847	Farmed at Sachem's Head, Guilford, Connecticut, where he employed Andrew Jackson Davis as landscape and architectural consultant; met Andrew Jackson Downing.
1848–54	Farmed at South Side, Staten Island, N. Y.
1850	Walking tour through British Isles and Western Europe.
1851	Visited Andrew Jackson Downing at Newburgh, N. Y.
1852–54	Traveled through the South as journalist for *The New York Times.*
1855–56	Editor and part-owner of *Putnam's Monthly Magazine.*
1856	*Putnam's* representative in London.
1857	*Putnam's* fails financially. Appointed Superintendent of Central Park, New York City.
1858	Appointed Architect-in-Chief of Central Park.
1859	Married widow of his younger brother, John Hull Olmsted—Mary Cleveland Perkins Olmsted. Trip to Europe to study European parks.
1860	Appointed, with Calvert Vaux, landscape architect to Commission laying out Manhattan Island north of 155th Street.
1861	Appointed Executive Secretary of the United States Sanitary Commission while on temporary leave of absence from Central Park; periodic visits to supervise Central Park.

163

1861–63	Urged efforts to provide emancipated Negroes with special educational and social opportunities.
1862–63	Co-founder of the Union League Club.
1863	Became director of Mariposa Mining Company, California.
	Resigned from United States Sanitary Commission and from Central Park position.
	Co-founder of *The Nation.*
1864	Honorary M.A. from Harvard University for service to United States Sanitary Commission.
	Appointed to Commission to establish Yosemite Park.
1865	Reappointed, with Vaux, Landscape Architect to the Board of Commissioners of Central Park.
	Appointed, with Vaux, to design a public park for Brooklyn.
1867	Honorary M.A. from Amherst College.
1869	Became aware of need to preserve Niagara Falls.
1870	Addressed the American Social Science Association at Lowell Institute, Boston.
	Appointed to coordinating committee for the improvement of Staten Island.
	Resigned, with Vaux, from Central Park Board of Commissioners because of political interference.
1871	Reappointed, with Vaux, landscape architect of Department of Parks, New York City.
1872	Appointed a Commissioner of the New York Department of Public Parks, and elected President and Treasurer of the Board. Vaux appointed landscape architect. Both men resigned and were reappointed—Olmsted as landscape architect and Vaux as consulting landscape architect.
	Dissolved partnership with Vaux.
1873	Traveled through New England and Canada with Henry H. Richardson.
1874	Collaborated with Jacob Weidenmann, a landscape architect.
1876–77	Political difficulties with New York City's Department of Public Parks again aggravated.
1877	Political difficulties over adoption of plan for the State Capitol Building at Albany.
1878	Removed from position with New York City Department of Public Parks.
	Traveled through Europe again.
	Principal figure in movement to preserve Niagara Falls.
1879	Engaged in campaign to preserve Niagara Falls.
1880	Addressed the American Social Science Association at Saratoga about public parks.
1883	Bought house at 99 Warren Street, Brookline, Massachusetts, which became permanent home and office.
	Concluded successful political campaign to preserve Niagara Falls.
1884	Participated in campaign to preserve the Adirondack region.
1887	Collaborated in the founding of periodical *Garden and Forest.*

164

	Appointed adviser to Board of Commissioners, Department of Parks, New York City—April 20–July 5, 1887.
1889	Henry Sargent Codman taken into partnership. Firm name becomes F. L. Olmsted & Co.
	Successfully opposed speeding track in Central Park.
	Successfully opposed establishing the World's Fair in Central Park.
1890	Elected member of Metropolitan Public Gardens Association (London).
1892	Honored for service to World's Columbian Exposition, Chicago.
1893	LL.D degrees from Harvard and Yale universities. Charles Eliot taken into partnership. The firm name becomes Olmsted, Olmsted & Eliot.
1895	Voluntary retirement from professional practice because of increased illness.
1896	Permanently incapacitated.
1903	Died August 28.

A CHRONOLOGICAL SELECTION OF FREDERICK LAW OLMSTED'S WORKS

1857	Collaborated with Calvert Vaux on competitive design for Central Park, New York City.
1858	Olmsted and Vaux's "Greensward" plan awarded first prize in open design competition for Central Park.
1865	Presented report for preservation and use of Yosemite Park, Calif. Published plan for Mountain View Cemetery, Oakland, Calif. (Fig. 24).
1866	Published plan, with Vaux, for Columbia Institute for the Deaf and Dumb (Gallaudet College), Washington, D.C. (Fig. 23). Published plan, with Vaux, for public park, San Francisco.
1866–67	Published plan, with Vaux, for Prospect Park, Brooklyn, N. Y. (Fig. 46).
	Published plan for a zoological collection, Central Park, New York City (this site is now occupied by the American Museum of Natural History; Fig. 18).
	Published plan, with Vaux, for college campus, Berkeley, Calif. (Fig. 4).
	Plan for national agricultural colleges.
	Plan for agricultural college, Amherst, Mass.
	Plan, with Vaux, for agricultural college, Orono, Maine.
1867	Prepared plan, with Vaux, for Fort Green[e] or Washington Park, Brooklyn, N. Y. (Fig. 48).
	Prepared plan, with Vaux, for Parade Ground, Brooklyn, N. Y. (Fig. 47).
	Prepared plan, with Vaux, for University of Maine.
1868	Published plan, with Vaux, for Eastern Parkway, Brooklyn, N. Y. (Fig. 50).
	Published plan, with Vaux, for public park, Newark.
	Published plan, with Vaux, for suburban community at Riverside, Ill. (Fig. 20).
	Prepared plan, with Vaux, for public parks (Delaware, The Parade, The Front), Buffalo, N. Y. (Figs. 52, 53, 54).
	Published plan, with Vaux, for City Park, Albany, N. Y.

166

1869	Advice sought on public park planning for Boston, Mass.
1870	Advised on design of Bushnell Park, Hartford, Conn.
1871	Published plan, with Vaux, for South Park(s), Chicago. (Fig. 58).
	Prepared "master-plan" for Staten Island with Elisha Harris, J. W. Trowbridge, and H. H. Richardson.
	Published plan, with Vaux, for Tarrytown Heights Land Company, Tarrytown, N. Y. (Fig. 21).
	Published plan, with Vaux, for Tompkins Park, Brooklyn (Fig. 49).
	Collaborated with H. H. Richardson on design of State Hospital (for mentally ill), Buffalo, N. Y. (Figs. 25, 52).
1872	Advised on site selection for Trinity College, Hartford.
1873	Prepared plan, with Vaux, for Morningside Park, New York City.
1874	Advice sought on public park for Montreal, Canada.
	Proposed plan of tree-planting for Washington, D.C. (Fig. 84).
	Proposed plan for Niagara Square, Buffalo, N. Y. (Fig. 55).
	Advised on site plan for Hartford Insane Retreat, Hartford.
1875	Proposed plans for design of United States Capitol, Washington, D.C.
	Prepared plan for Riverside Park and Avenue, New York City. (Fig. 77).
1876	Prepared plans for the laying out of the Twenty-third and Twenty-fourth Wards of New York City (The Bronx).
	Published proposal, with Leopold Eidlitz and H. H. Richardson, on plans to complete the New York State Capitol Building at Albany, N. Y. (Fig. 26).
	Prepared map of Buffalo for Philadelphia Centennial Exposition (Fig. 51).
	Revised plan for Niagara Square, Buffalo.
1877	Design map for Mount Royal Park, Montreal (Fig. 70).
	Proposed plan for transit routes in Twenty-third and Twenty-fourth wards of New York City (The Bronx; Fig. 78).
1878	Advised Charles S. Sargent on plan of Arnold Arboretum.
	Exhibited plan of Buffalo in Paris Exposition.
	Work in progress on United States Capitol.
1879	Proposed plan for development of Rockaway Point, N. Y., as a seaside resort.
	Proposed improvement of Back Bay, Boston (Fig. 39).
	Proposed plan for Arnold Arboretum, Boston (Fig. 41).
	Collaborated with Augustus St. Gaudens on siting of Farragut statue in Madison Square, New York City.
1880	Collaborated with H. H. Richardson on design of Ames Memorial Town Hall, North Easton, Mass. (Fig. 12).
	Collaborated with H. H. Richardson on the Boylston Bridge in the Boston Back Bay.
	Advice sought on design of Athletic Grounds of Yale University.
	Proposed plan for grounds of American Jockey Club, Jerome Park, Sheepshead Bay, Brooklyn.
	Collaborated with H. H. Richardson on design of Dr. John Bryant home, Cohasset, Mass.

1881	Collaborated with McKim, Mead and White on William Drew Washburn house, Minneapolis, Minn.
	Prepared plan for United States Commission of Fish and Fisheries, Washington, D.C.
	Collaborated with H. H. Richardson on Thomas Crane Public Library, Quincy, Mass.
	Advice to Merrymount Park Association, Quincy, Mass., on site for public park.
	Published plan for Mount Royal Park, Montreal.
	Further work on design of United States Capitol and grounds (Figs. 85, 86).
	Prepared plans for Anson Phelps Stokes estate, Newport, R. I.
	Prepared plan for Industrial Home School, Washington, D.C.
1881–82	Collaborated with H. H. Richardson on design of Mason Estate, Newport.
1882	Collaborated with H. H. Richardson on design of Boston & Albany Railroad station at Auburndale, Mass.
	Prepared plans on tree-planting in Washington, D.C.
	Prepared plan of Belle Isle Park, Detroit (Fig. 62).
	Design for Goddard Estate, Providence.
1883	Prepared preliminary design map for Belle Isle Park, Detroit (Fig. 63).
	Collaborated with H. H. Richardson on design of C. J. Hubbard estate, Weston, Mass.
	Collaborated with H. H. Richardson on design of Chestnut Hill Station, Boston & Albany Railroad.
	Completed study of campus plan for Lawrenceville School, Lawrenceville, N. J.
	Completed plans, in collaboration with architect Russell Sturgis, for Davis Estate, at Bateman's Point, Newport, R. I.
	Completed study of Cushing's Island, Portland, Maine, as site for summer colony.
	Completed plans for Bayley Estate, Newton, Mass.
	Completed plans for W. C. Cabot Estate, Brookline, Mass.
	Completed plans for public beach at Newport.
	Collaborated with architectural firm of Peabody and Stearns on Black Estate, Manchester, Mass.
	Advised on campus plan for Amherst College, including siting of gymnasium.
	Completed plan of grounds for Boston & Albany Railroad stations at Palmer, Brighton, Allston, and Newton.
1884	Advised on Telegraph Hill Properties, Newport.
	Advised on plan for Clifton Hill Properties, Brookline, Mass.
	Plan provided for Beardsley Park, Bridgeport (Fig. 44).
	Completed plan for J. W. Ellis estate, Newport.
	Proposed plans for West Roxbury Park and Wood Island Park, Boston.

168

Collaborated with H. H. Richardson on Robert Treat Paine estate, Waltham, Mass. (Figs. 9–11).

1886   Published plan for Franklin Park, Boston (Fig. 42).
Advised on campus plan for Groton School, Gordon, Mass., in collaboration with architect Robert Swain Peabody.
Agreed to work on plan for Leland Stanford Junior University, Palo Alto, Calif.
Prepared plan for grounds of Henry Clews estate, Newport.
Plan for a subdivision for the Vanderbilt family, Lenox, Mass.
Collaborated with H. H. Richardson on plan and design of Vanderbilt mausoleum, New Dorp, Staten Island, N. Y.
Report on condition of Golden Gate Park, San Francisco.

1887   Plan for arboretum and grounds of Webb Estate, Burlington, Vt.
Published plan, with Calvert Vaux, for improvement of the Niagara Reservation (Fig. 31).
Proposed plans with J. James R. Croes, for laying out the Newport Land Trust, as subdivision at Easton Point, Newport, R. I. (Fig. 73).
Revised general plan, with Calvert Vaux, for Morningside Park, New York City (Fig. 79).
Plan of interconnected park system for Boston (Fig. 32).

1888   Prepared plan with J. C. Olmsted, for public park in Pawtucket, R. I. (Fig. 80).
Prepared plans for South Park and parkways, Buffalo (Fig. 56).
Engaged by George W. Vanderbilt to advise and plan Biltmore estate, Asheville, N. C.
Provided design for Stanford University (Fig. 5).

1889   Advised on plans for State Capitol grounds, Montgomery, Ala.
Advised with Calvert Vaux, on Downing Park for Newburgh, N. Y.
Revised plan for Marine Park, Boston (Fig. 17).
Recommended that Lynn Woods, Lynn, Mass. be preserved and planned as public reservation (Fig. 19).
Report on Perry Park, Denver, Colo., as a resort community.
Proposed park plan for Rochester, N. Y.

1890   Advised on selection of Jackson Park, Chicago, as site for World's Columbian Exposition.

1891   Advised on plan for public park, Presque Isle, Mich.
Work on plan of World's Columbian Exposition.
Advised on land management for Elmwood Cemetery, Detroit, Mich.
Revised plan of Wood Island Park, Boston (Fig. 43).
Proposed plan for park system, Louisville.

1892   Advised further on design of site and planting of World's Columbian Exposition, Chicago.
Advised Park Commission of Milwaukee.
Published plan for Charlesbank, Boston (Fig. 16).
Proposed plan for Jamaica Park, Boston (Fig. 40).

1893	Advised on site plan for cotton exposition, Atlanta.
	Prepared plan for Seneca Park, Rochester, N. Y. (Fig. 82).
	Urged comprehensive planning for open spaces in Boston metropolitan region.
	Collaborated with William R. Ware on plan for campus of Columbia University.
1894	Advised on plan for Harlem River Driveway, New York City.
	Proposed plan for Lake Park, Milwaukee.
	Advised on management of Prospect Park, Brooklyn.
	Prepared report on park system for Cincinnati.
1895	Revised plan for Jackson Park, Chicago (Fig. 60).
	Advised on design of campus for Union College, Schenectady, N. Y.

SELECTED LIST
OF THE WRITINGS OF
FREDERICK LAW OLMSTED

In recent years, two anthologies of Olmsted's planning reports and pamphlet literature have been published: Albert Fein, ed., *Landscape into Cityscape: Frederick Law Olmsted's Plans for a Greater New York City* (Ithaca, N. Y., 1968); and S. B. Sutton, ed., *Civilizing American Cities: A Selection of Frederick Law Olmsted's Writings on City Landscapes* (Cambridge, Mass., 1971). Since these materials are scarce—not available in most libraries—this listing will indicate which anthology may be consulted. In addition, since several of Olmsted's books have been reissued, the most recent editions of these works have been indicated.

Books, Pamphlets and Periodical Literature

Olmsted, Frederick L. *Walks and Talks of an American Farmer in England.* Introduction by Alex L. Murray. Ann Arbor, 1967 (c. 1852).

————. *A Journey in the Seaboard Slave States, with Remarks on Their Economy.* New York, 1856.

————. *A Journey Through Texas; or, a Saddle-Trip on the Southwestern Frontier.* Edited by James Howard. Austin, 1962 (c. 1857).

————. *A Journey in the Back Country in the Winter of 1853–54.* New York, 1907 (c. 1860).

————. *The Cotton Kingdom: A Traveller's Observations on Cotton and Slavery in the American Slave States.* Edited, with an introduction, by Arthur M. Schlesinger. New York, 1966 (c. 1861).

————. ed. *Hospital Transports: A Memoir.* Boston, 1863.

————. "The Yosemite Valley and the Mariposa Big Trees, a Preliminary Report (1865)." Edited by Laura Wood Roper. *Landscape Architecture,* XLIII (October 1952), 12–25.

————. *Public Parks and the Enlargement of Towns.* Cambridge, Mass., 1870. Reprinted in *Civilizing American Cities.*

————. "Public Parks." *Garden,* X (March 25, 1876), 294–99.

————. "The Beginning of Central Park: A Fragment of Autobiography [ca. 1877]." Reprinted in *Landscape into Cityscape.*

171

————. "The Future of New York." *New York Daily Tribune*, December 28, 1879, p. 5.

————. *A Consideration of the Justifying Value of a Public Park.* Boston, 1881.

————. *The Spoils of the Park: With a Few Leaves from the Deep-laden Notebooks of "A Wholly Unpractical Man."* Detroit, 1882. Reprinted in *Landscape into Cityscape.*

————. "A Healthy Change in the Tone of the Human Heart (Suggestions to Cities)." *The Century Illustrated Monthly Magazine*, XXXII (October 1886), 963–64.

Olmsted, Frederick L., and Harrison, Jonathan Baxter. *Observations on the Treatment of Public Plantations, More Especially Relating to the Use of the Axe.* Boston, 1889.

Olmsted, Frederick L. "Parks, Parkways and Pleasure-Grounds." *Engineering Magazine*, IX (May 1895), 253–60.

Reports

Olmsted, Frederick L., and Vaux, Calvert. *Description of a Plan for the Improvement of Central Park, "Greensward."* New York, 1858 (reprinted, 1868). Reprinted in *Landscape into Cityscape.*

Olmsted, Frederick L. *Mariposa Estate, Manager's General Report.* New York, 1864.

————. *Report to the Trustees of the Mountain View Cemetery.* Privately printed, 1865.

————. *A Few Things to Be Thought of Before Proceeding to Plan Buildings for the National Agricultural Colleges.* New York, 1866.

Olmsted, Vaux & Co. *Preliminary Report to the Commissioners for Laying Out a Park in Brooklyn, New York: Being a Consideration of Circumstances of Site and Other Conditions Affecting the Design of Public Pleasure Grounds.* Brooklyn, 1866. Reprinted in *Landscape into Cityscape.*

————. *Preliminary Report in Regard to a Plan of Public Pleasure Grounds for the City of San Francisco.* New York, 1866. Partially reprinted in *Civilizing American Cities.*

————. *Report on the Columbia Institution for the Deaf and Dumb.* Washington, 1866.

————. *Report upon a Projected Improvement of the Estate of the College of California at Berkeley, near Oakland.* San Francisco, 1866. Partially reprinted in *Civilizing American Cities.*

————. *Architect's Report to the Board of Trustees of the College of Agriculture and the Mechanic Arts of the State of Maine.* 46th Legislature, House Document No. 57. Maine, 1867.

————. *Preliminary Report upon the Proposed Suburban Village at Riverside, near Chicago.* New York, 1868.

————. *Report to the Park Commissioners . . . for a Public Park for the City of Newark.* Trenton, 1868.

————. *Report of the Proposed City Park.* Albany, 1868.

————. *Preliminary Report Respecting a Public Park in Buffalo.* Buffalo, 1869.

————. *Report Accompanying Plan for Laying Out the South Park.* Chicago, 1871. Partially reprinted in *Civilizing American Cities.*

Olmsted, Frederick L., et al. *Report to the Staten Island Improvement Commission of a Preliminary Scheme of Improvements.* Reprinted in *Landscape into Cityscape.* 1871.

Olmsted, Frederick L., and Vaux, Calvert. *A Preliminary Study by the Landscape Architect(s) of a Design for the Laying Out of Morningside Park.* Document No. 50 of the Board of the Department of Public Parks of New York City, New York, 1873. Reprinted in *Landscape into Cityscape.*

Olmsted, Frederick L. *Report of the Landscape Architect upon the Construction of Riverside Park and Avenue.* Document No. 60 of the Board of the Department of Public Parks, New York, 1875. Reprinted in *Landscape into Cityscape.*

Olmsted, Frederick L.; Eidlitz, Leopold; and Richardson, H. H. *Report of the New Capitol Commission Relative to the Plans Submitted.* New York State Senate, Document 49, March 3, 1876.

Olmsted, Frederick L., and Croes, J. James R. *Document No. 72 of the Board of the Department of Public Parks: I. Preliminary Report of the Landscape Architect and the Civil and Topographical Engineer, upon the Laying Out of the Twenty-third and Twenty-fourth Wards; II. Report Accompanying a Plan for Laying Out that Part of the Twenty-fourth Ward, Lying West of the Riverdale Road.* Reprinted in *Landscape into Cityscape.* 1876.

————. *Document No. 75 of the Board of the Department of Public Parks: Report of the Landscape Architect and the Civil and Topographical Engineer, Accompanying a Plan for Local Steam Transit Routes in the Twenty-third and Twenty-fourth Wards.* Reprinted in *Landscape into Cityscape.* 1877.

Olmsted, Frederick L. "Report of a Preliminary Survey of Rockaway Point (1879)." Reprinted in *Landscape into Cityscape.*

————. *Mount Royal, Montreal.* New York, 1881. Partially reprinted in *Civilizing American Cities.*

————. ". . . Paper Relating to the Trees, Shrubs, and Plants in the United States Capitol Ground, and an Index of the Same Together with Some Observations upon the Planting and Care of Trees in the District of Columbia," in *Annual Report of the Architect [Edward Clark] of the United States Capitol for the Fiscal Year Ending June 30, 1882.*

————. *The Park for Detroit: . . . Belle Isle Scheme.* Privately printed, 1882.

————. *Improvement of Easton's Beach.* Boston, 1883.

————. *Belle Isle: After One Year* (n.p., 1884).

————. *Notes on the Plan of Franklin Park and Related Matters.* Boston, 1886.

Olmsted, Frederick L., and Vaux, Calvert. *General Plan for the Improvement of Morningside Park, with Report.* New York, 1887. Reprinted in *Landscape into Cityscape.*

————. *General Plan for the Improvement of Niagara Reservation.* New York, 1887.

Olmsted, Frederick L., and Olmsted, John Charles. *Plan of Public Recreation Grounds for the City of Pawtucket.* Boston, 1888.

173

————. *The Projected Park and Parkways of the South Side of Buffalo. Two Reports by the Landscape Architects.* Buffalo, 1888. Partially reprinted in *Civilizing American Cities.*

————. "Landscape Architects' Report," *Beardsley Park.* Boston, 1889.

Olmsted, Frederick Law, & Company. "Report on Parks and Parkmaking." In *First Annual Report of the Board of Park Commissioners of the City of Louisville.* Louisville, 1891, 25–27.

Olmsted, Frederick L. "A Report Upon the Landscape Architecture of the Columbian Exposition to the American Institute of Architects." *American Architect and Building News,* XLI (September 9, 1893), 151–54.

————. "The Landscape Architecture of the World's Columbian Exposition." *The Inland Architect and News Record,* XXII (September 1893), 18–22.

BACKGROUND BIBLIOGRAPHY

Brooks, Van Wyck. *The Flowering of New England, 1815–1865.* New York: E. P. Dutton & Co., 1936.

Burchard, John Ely, and Bush-Brown, Albert. *The Architecture of America.* Boston: Little, Brown and Co., 1961.

Callow, James T. *Kindred Spirits: Knickerbocker Writers and American Artists, 1807–1855.* Chapel Hill: University of North Carolina Press, 1967.

Chadwick, George F. *The Park and the Town: Public Landscape in the 19th and 20th Centuries.* New York: Frederick A. Praeger, 1966.

Clark, H. F. *The English Landscape Garden.* London: Pleiades Books Limited, 1948.

Fein, Albert, ed. *Landscape into Cityscape: Frederick Law Olmsted's Plans for a Greater New York City.* Ithaca: Cornell University Press, 1967.

Fitch, James Marston. *American Building.* 2d ed. rev. and enl. 2 vols. Vol. I: *The Historical Forces That Shaped It.* Boston: Houghton Mifflin, 1966. Vol. II: *The Environmental Forces That Shape It.* Boston: Houghton Mifflin, 1972.

Flexner, James Thomas. *That Wilder Image: The Painting of America's Nature School from Thomas Cole to Winslow Homer.* Boston: Little, Brown and Co., 1962.

Harris, Neil. *The Artist in American Society: The Formative Years 1790–1860.* New York: George Braziller, Inc., 1966.

Hitchcock, Henry-Russell. *The Architecture of H. H. Richardson and His Times.* 3d ed. Cambridge, Mass.: M.I.T. Press, 1966.

Hofstadter, Richard. *The Age of Reform: From Bryan to F.D.R.* New York: Alfred A. Knopf, Inc., 1955.

Huth, Hans. *Nature and the American: Three Centuries of Changing Attitudes.* Berkeley and Los Angeles: University of California Press, 1957.

Kaufmann, Edgar, Jr. *The Rise of an American Architecture.* New York: Frederick A. Praeger, 1970.

Matthiessen, Francis Otto. *American Renaissance: Art and Expression in the Age of Emerson and Whitman.* 4th ed. London: Oxford University Press, 1949.

Maxwell, William Q. *Lincoln's Fifth Wheel: The Political History of the United States Sanitary Commission.* New York: Longmans, Green & Co., 1956.

Miller, Lillian B. *Patrons and Patriotism.* Chicago: University of Chicago Press, 1966.

Mumford, Lewis, ed. *Roots of Contemporary American Architecture.* New York: Reinhold, 1952.

Reed, Henry Hope, and Duckworth, Sophia. *Central Park: A History and a Guide.* New York: Clarkson N. Potter, Inc., 1967.

Rosenberg, Charles E. *The Cholera Years: The United States in 1832, 1849, and 1866.* Chicago: University of Chicago Press, 1962.

Schuyler, Montgomery. *American Architecture and Other Writings.* Edited by William H. Jordy and Ralph Coe. 2 vols. Cambridge: Harvard University Press, 1961.

Stein, Roger B. *John Ruskin and Aesthetic Thought in America, 1840–1900.* Cambridge, Mass.; Harvard University Press, 1967.

Sutton, S. B., ed. *Civilizing American Cities: A Selection of Frederick Law Olmsted's Writings on City Landscapes.* Cambridge, Mass.: M.I.T. Press, 1971.

Tunnard, Christopher. *The Modern American City.* Princeton: D. Van Nostrand Company, Inc., 1968.

176

INDEX

Figure numbers refer to plates or to captions, according to the context.

SOURCES OF ILLUSTRATIONS

Numbers refer to figure numbers.

The American Architect and Building News, North Easton, Mass., H. H. Richardson, Architect, Pl. II: 12.

Boston Public Library: 38.

Chicago Historical Society: 57, 59.

Detroit Public Library, Burton Historical Collection: 61–63.

Dumbarton Oaks, Garden Library: 23, 24, 31, 45–48, 50–56, 58, 76–79, 95, 96, 98, 103.

Harvard Graduate School of Design Library negative: **2, 5, 17, 18, 22, 28,** 42, 73, 80, 104; "Achievement of Frederick Law Olmsted (1822–1903)," 1964: 3; John Cordis Baker, ed., *American Country Homes and Their Gardens,* Philadelphia, House and Garden, The J. C. Winston Co., 1906, p. 124: 29; Boston, Board of Commissioners of the Department of Parks, 5th Annual Report, 1879: 41; 11th Annual Report, 1885: 39; 17th Annual Report, 1892: 43; 18th Annual Report, 1893: 40; 19th Annual Report, 1894: 97; 29th Annual Report, 1904: 105; Department of Parks, *Notes on the Plan of Franklin Park and Related Matters,* 1886: 37; Bridgeport, Conn., Park Commission, Beardsley Park, 1884: 44; Brooklyn, New York, Commissioners of Prospect Park, 11th Annual Report: 49; Ihna T. Frary, *They Built the Capitol,* Books for Libraries, Inc., 1940: 86; *House and Garden,* February, 1906: 70–72; March, 1906: 85; Johnson, Johnson and Roy, Inc., *A Study of Future Development for Jackson Park,* May 31, 1966: 60; Minutes and Documents of Central Park, New York City, year ending April 2, 1873: 91. New York City, Commissioners of Central Park, 1st Annual Report, 1857: 88; 3rd Annual Report, 1860: 89, 92; 5th Annual Report, 1862: 93, 94, 99; 7th Annual Report, 1863: 100, 101; 9th Annual Report, 1865: 90: 10th Annual Report, 1866: 19; Report on a City Plan for the Municipalities of Oakland and Berkeley, 1915: 4; U.S. Congress, 58th, 2nd Session, Doc. 4585, 1904: 84.

Nathan Mortimer Hawkes, *In Lynn Woods with Pen and Camera,* 1893, Lynn, Mass.: 20.

Henry–Russell Hitchcock, *The Architecture of H. H. Richardson and His Times,* Archon Books, 1961: 13, 25.

Louisville Public Library, Park Commissioners, 1st Annual Report, 1891: 64, 65; 2nd Annual Report, 1892; 15, 16, 66–68.

Theodore Tremain McCrosky, *et al., Surging Cities,* Greater Boston Development Committee, 1948: 33–35.

Blake McKelvey, *Rochester the Flower City, 1855–1890,* Harvard University Press, 1949, p. 236: 81.

Museum of the City of New York: 102.

New-York Historical Society: 6, 74, 87.

New York Public Library: 7, 8; the I. N. Phelps Stokes Collection, Prints Division, Astor, Lenox, and Tilden Foundations: 36, 69, 75, 83.

Olmsted Associates, Inc., Brookline, Mass.: 1, 20, 27, 32, 82.

St. Johnsbury Athenaeum, St. Johnsbury, Vermont: 30.

Thomas M. Paine: 9–11.

Edward Teitelman, Photography: 14, 26.